GET THE CALLBACK

The Art of Auditioning for Musical Theatre

Jonathan Flom

THE SCARECROW PRESS, INC.

Lanham, Maryland • Toronto • Plymouth, UK

SCARECROW PRESS, INC.

Published in the United States of America
by Scarecrow Press, Inc.
A wholly owned subsidiary of
The Rowman & Littlefield Publishing Group, Inc.
4501 Forbes Boulevard, Suite 200, Lanham, Maryland 20706
www.scarecrowpress.com

Estover Road
Plymouth PL6 7PY
United Kingdom

British Library Cataloguing in Publication Information Available

Library of Congress Cataloging-in-Publication Data

Flom, Jonathan, 1977–
    Get the callback : the art of auditioning for musical theatre / Jonathan Flom.
        p. cm.
    Includes index.
    ISBN 978-0-8108-6398-9 (cloth : alk. paper) — ISBN 978-0-8108-6918-9 (pbk. : alk.
paper) — ISBN 978-0-8108-6953-0 (ebook)
1. Musicals—Auditions. 2. Acting—Auditions. I. Title.
MT956.F56 2009
792.602'8—dc22   2009010535

∞ ™ The paper used in this publication meets the minimum requirements of
American National Standard for Information Sciences—Permanence of Paper
for Printed Library Materials, ANSI/NISO Z39.48-1992.
Manufactured in the United States of America.

CONTENTS

PREFACE

Many books have been published over the years that offer instruction and insight into the unique and terrifying world of auditioning for the theatre. A handful of these publications pertain to the musical theatre stage—an area with extremely specific demands that merits the dedication of an entire book. Of those available publications, I have found that very few are current, concise, and complete. When I studied musical theatre as a performer in Penn State's BFA program in the late '90s, we were given a guide for learning the technique of auditioning, with the caveat that some of the information might already be outdated or disputable but with the understanding that it contained a large proportion of useful information. In 2004, when I began to teach the auditions course at Penn State, I looked at several books and found that my old college text was still the most relevant.

As I created my syllabus, I took the time to divide the manual's chapters into three categories: (1) the absolutely true and useful; (2) the questionable, which students could debate in class; and (3) the outdated or arguably incorrect information, which we would skip.

Later, while preparing to teach my class in Chicago, I lamented that there wasn't a single book that comprised everything I feel any working actor or professional-in-training ought to know about auditioning for musicals. Why must I always offer someone else's book as a jumping-off point, only to supplement the instructional material with what I have found to be true over the years as a director and an instructor? The logical conclusion I drew was to take a stab at writing my own guide to auditioning.

As I embarked on this project, I realized that one fundamental philosophy seems to be lacking in every sourcebook I read. While these guides preach methodologies designed to help actors achieve success, the results used to measure success are either unidentified or misdirected. When not explicitly stated, the assumption is that an actor attends an audition with the objective of being cast. I believe this is a mistake. Actors are not cast based on their initial audition; they are hired after a callback (or a series of callbacks). Thus, the goal of an audition for actors should always be to show themselves at their best, and the most fortuitous result would be to earn a callback. With this subtle shift in mindset, actors are concerned less with what they are "looking for" and focus instead on presenting the best they have to offer.

I have always been fascinated by the audition process. As I alluded earlier, my first degree was in musical theatre performance, so I have a great deal of experience on the "red X." As I moved through my undergraduate years, however, I became increasingly interested in directing. I struggled in my acting classes simply because I was too conscious of what I (and everyone else) was doing in a given scene; I was always trying to see the big picture as opposed to living in the moment. I found my niche when I began to direct plays.

Over the years, I have been "behind the table" for productions ranging from student-run college projects to university main-stage shows to hole-in-the-wall guerilla theatre in New York to major regional theatre productions around the country—not to mention my years of college recruitment auditions. In all of these venues, certain theories and methods of practice hold true for success. In this book, I will outline those theories and methods in as clear and practical a format as possible.

Art is not something that one can learn from a how-to book. You can't read this or any publication and suddenly find yourself a talented performer at the end. Art is something that is inborn. Many people say success in the arts comes not from the desire to be an artist but from the *need* to be an artist. They say if you don't need to do art to breathe, then you should find yourself another career. I don't have to provide the staggering odds that are stacked against any performer's chances of gainful employment. Suffice it to say if you can do anything else, you should.

But this book is for those who have decided that they do, in fact, need to do it. This book is for those who have decided they are ready to make a commitment to a life in the theatre, no matter in what stage of that commitment they find themselves—be it preparing for a training program or working on Broadway. As I said, the same guidelines and techniques apply at any level. But you must be prepared to invest a great deal of time as well as money, not to mention a whole lot of heart and soul, to find success in the theatre.

In the chapters that follow, I will walk you through the entire process of auditioning for musical theatre. We will begin with everything that you need to do before you even walk into the room. I will then outline tips for the actual audition itself. I have yet to find a book that examines what happens after the audition—callbacks and (hopefully) job offers. We will talk about those situations as well. And, since I have spent so much of my career as a college recruiter and teacher, I will offer a chapter dealing specifically with advice on auditioning for college and university training programs.

Before you proceed, there are just a couple of things you should keep in mind. First of all, no method will guarantee you casting results. Sometimes no matter how talented or good-looking you are, no matter how much you charm them when you go into that room, they simply have someone else in mind for the part. Following the guidelines I set out in this book will simply increase your odds by helping you appear more professional and more confident. Sometimes the lazy, sloppy, underprepared person will get the job over you. Remember, there is an intangible element of luck and timing in this industry. But I cannot tell you what a breath of fresh air it is for a director when someone comes in polished, put together, and ready for whatever we throw at him. Following this method will give you an edge in that respect.

Also, keep in mind that even as a working actor, you will spend the largest percentage of your time auditioning for other work (even Broadway performers go on auditions weekly). Essentially, then, your job *is* auditioning! You need to embrace the audition as an opportunity. When you're between gigs, auditioning may be the only performing you do for a long stretch of time. Ed Linderman, a New York composer/musical director and a long-time mentor of mine, always told us that auditioning is "your daily chance to perform. It's the (insert your name here) show." So you mustn't treat it lightly.

Too many training programs, it seems, spend two to four years teaching students how to perform—how to act, how to sing, how to dance. Usually, they are given the chance to put it all together and actually appear in live productions. Of course, it is to be expected that auditioning will be part and parcel to this whole experience, but usually the audition is just a means to an end. The director needs to find a cast, so auditions are held. Although many schools offer a course on audition technique, the vast majority of training time is focused on actual performance skills. This lack of attention to the importance of auditioning could be the reason that auditioning is approached so fearfully by actors, young and old alike. People who have no fear on stage in productions often tend to shut down and freeze when they are auditioning. Why is this? Because they don't rehearse for the audition the way they rehearse for a production.

And so, I urge you to immediately cease regarding the audition process as a means to an end and try to think of it as a complete performance event in and of itself. If you can logically imagine yourself rehearsing and polishing a play or musical in order to be prepared to perform for an audience, then you can treat the audition process with the same respect. If you get enthusiastic and high from the rush of performing in front of an opening night crowd, try to find that same positive rush from auditioning. And, as the great Toronto film acting coach David Rotenberg says, if all else fails, "act like you're happy to be here! If you can't make us believe that, then you're dead in the water."

ACKNOWLEDGMENTS

This book has been a joyous project for me because I love the theatre and I love the audition process. However, it would never have been possible to consider such an undertaking without the continuing support of my friends, mentors, and family, not to mention the producers who have hired me and the actors I have hired (and not hired) who have instilled in me the knowledge and experiences I have set forth in these pages. It is my privilege to thank the following people specifically for their contributions:

- Mark Olsen and Lori Sessions for their suggestions and encouragement
- Ed Linderman for teaching me the joy of auditioning
- Cary Libkin for taking a young director under his wing years ago
- Penn State School of Theatre faculty for all the training and the constant support
- Mary Saunders and Mollye Otis for tips from the voice experts
- Tom Albert, Susan Russell, and Todd Courson for helping to shepherd the book to publishers
- Melissa Carlile-Price, Morgan Faulkner, and Shaina Taub for their stories
- Julie Foster, Michele Dunleavy, Kimberlee Johnson, Zachary Durand, Tom Albert, Carolyn Coulson-Grigsby, and Sharon Durand for being readers

- my Shenandoah Conservatory students for being my guinea pigs
- Renée Camus and Scarecrow Press for making this project a reality

And finally, to my "network":

- Julio A. Matos Jr. and Matt Toronto for being copilots
- the Penn State Musical Theatre Eight for never-ending friendship
- Jennifer and Pedro for love, encouragement, laughs, partnership, adventures . . .
- my parents, Janice and Michael Flom, for never once telling me to become a dentist

BEFORE THE AUDITION

HOLDING THE BABY

You probably know that a director's job begins long before the first day of casting. By the time the notices are posted, the director has spent months, sometimes years, of her life preparing for the moment when she will start meeting actors. I always equate the casting of actors in a show with the idea of babysitting a newborn child. The play is the director's baby. She has invested time and passion and love into helping the little project develop. Often, there are also producers who are investing large sums of money as well. When audition time arrives, the director must decide whom she trusts to "hold the baby." Are you trustworthy and reliable? Will you help foster the child's development and ensure success?

Choosing actors is an equal mix of excitement and angst: the director may find the perfect person, or she may have to settle for something other than her vision. An actor should be sensitive to the director's position in regard to the audition process. Realize that no director in his or her right mind hopes that you will come into the room and fail. We are all hoping that you walk in and blow us all away! We want you to be exactly what we envisioned; better yet, we want you to show us that you can be much better than we imagined. As I write this very chapter, I am sitting in a lonely room waiting for actors to show up for my open casting call for a production of *The Last Five Years* in the Chicago suburbs. A half hour has passed and not one single actor has come through the door (fortunately or unfortunately, affording me the time to write what you are now reading). With each passing hour, I will become more and more desirous of someone to come in and nail a reading for me. I may get desperate. Although this is not usually the case (Broadway auditions, for example, often have upwards of 300 people show up for open calls), you can understand how a director sees the casting process. She may be more nervous than you, in fact. You may not need the job, but she *needs* to cast the show.

All that said, you must prove that you are worthy of holding the baby. The only surefire way to do that is to prepare. Prepare for anything and everything. When you walk in the door, you must communicate to the production team that you are not only talented enough for the role but also tenacious, enthusiastic, and above all professional. Ed Linderman instructs students to "convince the people behind the table that putting you in their show will make them look good." I cannot think of better advice to offer an actor. It's completely unselfish. And it's the absolute opposite of the typical "I need a job" mentality with which most actors regard auditions. More on that notion later.

Obviously, training is of the utmost importance for survival in the theatre. A performing artist, in particular a musical theatre performer, must be a well-trained actor, singer, and dancer to compete in today's market. And while this book is in no way intended to be a book on acting, singing, or dance technique, I can offer some sound advice that will enhance your overall audition presentation package: your "you" show.

First of all, *act everything*. Do not for a moment think that acting is for the monologue and reading auditions, and leave your vocal and dance skills to handle everything else. We want to see you invest fully in the character you are portraying whether the story you are telling is through dance, spoken word, or sung lyrics. This is, after all, what good musical theatre is about. Assuming you are taking scene study classes in high school, college, or in a city somewhere, you should be sure to apply everything you are learning about acting and being truthful, etcetera, to every song you sing and every piece of choreographed movement you execute. Furthermore, to that end, I highly recommend *A Practical Handbook for the Actor* by Melissa Bruder et al. (Vintage, 1986). It lays out in simple and concise terms a vocabulary and a technique for actors at any level. My Meisner-based training employed this guide, and it has served me well, both as an actor and as a director/instructor.

Second, continued vocal training and coaching is of the utmost importance all the way through one's career. Once you learn a technique for supporting with breath and controlling your voice, you need to practice regularly under guidance. Performing in shows and auditioning is not enough, since no one will be attending to your vocal needs and issues directly, apart from the musical director, who is only concerned about how you sing the particular score on which you are working. You need to invest time and money in someone who will help you continue to grow and develop as a singer, and who will hopefully help you learn to infuse acting into your song presentation. Not to mention that having a vocal coach to play piano for you eliminates the trap of original cast recordings. But we will discuss that in more detail soon.

Finally, take dance classes. Take any dance class you can. Musical theatre was once known for its use of ballet in the age of Agnes DeMille. Later, Jerome Robbins became the predominate choreographer, employing more of a jazz dance style. Bob Fosse created a unique, isolation/movement–based dance technique that infiltrated the ranks of Broadway shows in the 1970s. Tap has always been part of the musical theatre vocabulary. And now, more and more frequently, shows are infusing blends of modern, urban, and cultural dance styles into their productions. The bottom line is, the more you know, the better off you will be. You may not consider yourself a great dancer, but I promise you that if you want a career in musical theatre, having a solid (and constantly growing) set of dance fundamentals will be invaluable to you along your path. So take a social dance class. Learn some modern. Why not go to the local town hall on swing or salsa dance lesson night? And again, act the heck out of every piece of choreography you are asked to execute.

The Idol Truth

I think the popularity of reality "talent" shows such as *American Idol* has created a vast misperception as to the nature and purpose of auditioning. People's (a cappella) auditions are put on display for judgment and mockery by the three stern judges. Ratings are particularly high when a tone-deaf ignoramus is humiliated for public enjoyment. However, I assure you this is not what you should expect to encounter in the real world of auditions, professional or amateur.

This is not to say you won't have frustrating or uncomfortable experiences along the way, but by and large, auditions are a means to an end. A director or artistic team wishes to find the ideal cast for their project, and when you walk in the room they hope you will wow them.

You will almost always find that piano accompaniment will be provided (unless otherwise stated in the casting ad), so you should not prepare to sing a cappella. Once I actually had a young girl show up at an audition and sing unaccompanied with her iPod playing in her ears. This is not the best choice by far! Even for community, high school, and other amateur auditions, you should do your best to follow the guidelines set out in this book and look professional.

INVESTING IN YOUR CAREER

As I mentioned before, and as you'll hear over and over again, a career in the arts is an investment. You cannot hope to be successful if you are unwilling to spend the time and money it takes to compete. Assuming you have already committed to classes in acting, singing, and dancing, your next move is to get yourself a fantastic headshot. The headshot can range in price from as low as $250 to upwards of $1,000. While the amount of money you spend on photos is not necessarily in direct proportion to the quality of the shots, it is nonetheless too important a factor in your career to leave in the hands of an amateur photographer.

I cannot tell you the number of times a student has asked me to look at her new "headshots"—pictures that her father took in the backyard—and advise which one she should use. My answer is always "None." A photographer requires a very specific understanding of the theatre industry to shoot actors' headshots. While you may look extremely pretty or handsome in the pictures your cousin took with her new digital camera, chances are your pictures will not even come close to being in the same class as the myriad others that come across a director's desk during the casting process. And chances are, your unprofessional shots will wind up in the express lane to the "round file."

Now being completely realistic, it is silly to imagine a high school student auditioning for colleges spending the kind of money that a seasoned professional would spend on photos, especially considering that the younger you are, the more you will change, and the more frequently you will need to get new headshots. However, an actor at any level with professional aspirations should get herself at least a minimally passable headshot. Although some colleges and community theatre auditions will not require it, it is another way of giving you a professional edge and showing that you are serious and committed to your career as a performer. In a later chapter, I will go more in depth on what to look for in a headshot. But for now, let us agree that it is a necessary and logical expense. Along with the headshot, of course, comes the résumé. I will discuss the art of crafting a polished résumé in a later chapter as well.

One other important tool of the trade that no performer should be without is a tape recorder. It can be digital or old-fashioned reel-to-reel; I have even seen students plugging in a microphone and recording directly to their iPod or phone. A tape recorder is a necessary investment for call-backs or rehearsals during which music will be taught which actors will be expected to learn quickly. Although sight-reading is an incredibly valuable skill included in most good training programs, a recording device is a great way to capture exactly what the musical director is listening for in the song he is teaching you. Having one with you shows that you are prepared and serious about your work.

Finally, you'll need your materials for a repertoire book, which I will discuss in detail in the next chapter. And I think every serious actor should also have a journal or a blank book. This way, you can keep track of every director, casting director, choreographer, and producer you audition for. You should make a note of every project you go in for: who was behind the table, what you sang or what monologue you performed, and any reaction you received from them, including whether or not they called you back. This way, when you go in for those artists again, you will know what works or what doesn't work. It will show signs of a savvy, professional performer.

FINDING THE WORDS TO SAY

One of the most common questions I am asked by students of all ages is how and where to find good material. As far as finding monologues is concerned, I will offer first this single suggestion: *Get rid of the monologue books*. The best thing you can do as an aspiring actor is to be reading and seeing plays constantly. This is where you will find your sources for audition pieces. Go to the theatre and bring a scratch pad with you. Sit in a bookstore with a great drama section and read, read, read. Even if you consider yourself "just" a musical theatre performer, you will need monologues ready at the helm at all times. Believe it or not, many musical theatre auditions call for monologues as well as songs.

Monologue books are generally filled with contentless performance pieces. The characters are not fully developed. More often than not, the speeches are either designed to bring the house down with laughter or to extract painful tears from the listener as the character talks about his dead best friend, sibling, or parent. And generally, these pieces fail on either front: The comedic ones are almost never funny, and the only thing painful about the sad ones is that they seem to go on forever.

If you are serious about being an actor, you need to search out plays that contain roles that are appropriate to your specific age and type. You need to find plays that speak to you somehow, so that you can fully invest in an understanding of the character and his world. You should be able to discuss in detail the needs and actions of any character whom you are portraying, and the only way this is possible is if the monologue is part of a fully-developed play that you have read and comprehended.

Admittedly, some directors do not consider monologue book pieces to be as great a pet peeve as I do. Doing one will not necessarily keep you from being cast. However, coming in with an appropriate piece from a real play will only enhance your appearance of being a professional and increase the odds of the director wanting to work with you. *It will give you an edge.*

If you feel you must use a monologue book as a source of age-appropriate character material, be sure the speech is from an actual play, and read the play before performing the piece. And for goodness sake, do not write your own monologue!

You may have noticed that all my talk of monologues has stipulated that they be from plays. I am being very specific about that. Other common sources of monologues for young actors include films, television episodes, and Internet websites. Again, there are some directors who won't care what the material is, so long as you perform it well; however, many theatre practitioners are very particular about actors choosing material from dramatic literature. So in order to avoid unpleasant reactions, why not just find all your source material in plays? There are certainly enough out there to give you limitless options.

The Internet often leads you to more contentless pieces written as performance art, similar to the monologue book. And the danger in film and TV monologues is that you will be performing a piece indelibly connected with the specific actor who originated the role on film. You'll either be imitating her or not living up to how she delivered the speech. Either way, I feel it's not a risk worth taking. Film monologues should only be used in film auditions.

When it comes to finding music, I offer similar council. Shy away from anthologies and collections of Great Songs for Musical Theatre Whatevers. Go see musicals, read libretti (musical theatre scripts), find characters for which you are castable and sing their songs. The anthologies in and of themselves are not as bad as monologue books—in fact, they can be quite helpful tools for finding published sheet music. Here's the trap, though: Too often, actors rely on the books alone to be their sources of material. They do not understand what the play is about or who the character is (e.g., the 17-year-old girl who sings "Broadway Baby," a song from *Follies* written for a woman in her 70s). Like the bad monologues, these audition songs become contentless, and thus they are poor choices.

In conjunction with the dangers of the anthology, let me also warn you about the trap of original cast recordings. Many performers rely on the cast album to learn their music for auditions. I can offer you several reasons why this is a bad idea. First of all, you are not learning the song; rather, you are learning a particular actor's version of that song. Even if that actor sings the piece note perfect (which is not usually the case), he still has his own nuances and interpretations. We can assume he has made his own character choices, which will then inform his delivery of the song. You are much more likely to sing the song as you learned it, through that particular artist's style, as opposed to the literal way it is notated on the page (I have yet to hear a song from Stephen Schwartz's *Wicked* in an audition—all I've heard are imitations of Idina Menzel and Kristin Chenoweth). Furthermore, you will often find that the keys are changed from the original score when they are published in vocal selection and anthology books. All too often, actors learn a song along with a CD only to discover *in the audition room* that their vocal selections book is written in a key way too high or way too low for them. Embarrassing, I assure you.

This all relates back to my insistence that a career in the arts involves expenditures galore. You must be willing to pay a coach or an accompanist to sit down and play through all of your music with you (unless you play piano yourself, another very valuable skill). You can then employ your sight-reading skills and your tape recorder to make this process much easier and more efficient. Experience tells me that this is the only truly reliable way to learn music and avoid humiliation of the sort I just mentioned.

As long as you are willing to learn your music directly from the written page, I will retract my admonition to avoid cast recordings, and I will instead suggest them as another valuable way of finding material. When I am discovering new musicals, I like to sit down with the libretto and the cast recording and listen to the songs as I come to them in my reading. However, once I am committed to directing or performing in a project, I cease listening to the soundtrack to avoid its influencing my own personal artistic choices. This is the path I recommend to you.

Whether you are just beginning to collect repertoire material or you have a six-inch-thick binder full of music, I would suggest that you consider creating two compilations: Let us call them your "A" book and your "B" book. The "A" book is the one that goes everywhere with you (a performer should never be without music; you never know when a performance opportunity may arise). This is the book that is not too heavy to schlep around in a back-pack or briefcase. It contains a variety of songs from varying genres, decades, and styles, but generally not more than 15 to 20 pieces. Most importantly, *you must know every song in this book by rote and be ready to sing any of them.*

If you have songs in your book that you once copied and intended to learn, take them out until you've learned them. If you have songs that you hate to sing or that you are not comfortable performing, take them out. I cannot tell you how often an actor will come in to audition, give her music to the accompanist, and do the song she prepared. The director will take an interest in her, but the song she chose just isn't bringing out what he needs to see, so he asks if she has something else. Guess what the accompanist does? He thumbs through that actor's rep book and calls out some titles to the director (after all, the accompanist very likely knows what the director would prefer to hear). If the actor is not able to sing something in that book, it's egg on her face. So, while it is wise to have a widely varied book cover-ing every imaginable style of song, it is counterproductive to you unless you can sing any of the songs at the drop of a hat. *I would prefer you have four choices—a contemporary ballad, a contemporary up-tempo, a standard ballad, and a standard up-tempo—that you know perfectly.*

The purpose of the "B" book is to house all of that other music you have amassed that doesn't need to be carted along with you everywhere. This includes songs you are learning or plan to learn, songs that are not perfor-mance-ready aces for you, songs you are tired or bored with, and specialty songs that only need inclusion for specific auditions. The "B" book is the one you take to your voice lessons and coachings. This is your private work-in-progress book. No accompanist in an audition situation should ever get his hands on this binder.

In addition, you should be prepared to sing from shows you've done; if you aren't comfortable singing a role you've done in your career, remove it from your résumé. Anything listed on there must be considered fair game at an audition.

In the chapter that follows, I will go into much greater detail on building and maintaining a working repertoire book.

FINDING THE CHANCE TO SAY
THE WORDS YOU'VE FOUND

When I first moved to New York, the Internet was up and running, but most theatre jobs were still only posted in print. You had to turn to *Back*

Stage or *Show Business* to find audition notices. Now, however, theatre has gone techno, and most openings for performers can be accessed on the web. Furthermore, with the vast accessibility of the Internet, theatres all over the country are inclined to post audition information online, so you can hear about casting calls from the MUNY in St. Louis just as easily as you can be informed about Broadway cattle calls. Some websites you may find helpful include

> www.backstage.com
> www.backstagejobs.com
> www.performink.com (Chicago)
> www.playbill.com
> www.showbusinessweekly.com
> www.tcg.org (ArtSearch)
> www.upta.org

And those are just for starters. I'm certain that by the time this book is published there will be at least a dozen other online sources for gigs. Use Google—it's your friend!

Wherever you find your casting call ads or your college audition requirements, it is incumbent upon you as a professional to read carefully. If it's a show, what role(s) are they casting? If it's a season, what shows? How do you get an audition? Do you show up, sign up, or submit a headshot and résumé by mail? What are they asking to hear at auditions? Do they want one song, two songs, song cuttings, etcetera? There is a great deal of information contained in a casting ad and you need to understand, interpret, and read between the lines. Misinterpreting a call or arriving underprepared will make you look very unprofessional and take away your edge.

My first job when I moved to New York was editing and typing casting call ads for *Back Stage*. It was my job to put every advertisement into the standard format and to make sure the theatres were all, at the very least, legitimate. (As a smart actor, you should realize that a casting call for some Podunk theatre in a burned-out warehouse in Brooklyn is going to read as legit and professional as an Off-Broadway Equity casting. There are a lot of scams and scummy theatres out there, and you should rely on word-of-mouth and the Internet to stay informed.) Let's take a look at a hypothetical example and see what we can glean:

The Last Five Years, **Pawtucket Players**

Fri. June 29 & Sat. June 30 from 12 p.m. to 3 p.m. at Pawtucket High Auditorium, 5 Main St.

The Pawtucket Players, a 30-year-old regional theatre in historic Pawtucket, RI, are casting for a summer production of Jason Robert Brown's The Last Five Years. Bill Jones, dir.; Sadie Hawkings, mus. dir. Rehearsals begin July 1. Performances will run from July 22 through August 13. Auditions will be held Friday, June 29, and Saturday, June 30, from 12 p.m. to 3 p.m. at the Pawtucket High School auditorium. Bring pix and résumé and prepare two contrasting 16-bar cuttings from contemporary musical theatre. Both roles are paid ($350/wk.), plus housing included. For more information, visit www.pawplayers.net. **Equity Guest Artist Contract Available.**

Seeking: Jamie—male; 26-30; confident Jewish man, on his way up; charming; pop-rock bari-tenor voice range. Cathy—female; 23-28; sweet gentile girl, very vulnerable but with the ability to display inner strength when tested; belter. **EQUITY/NON-EQUITY PERFORMERS.**

And there you have it, a casting call for young men and women—simple and concise. So let's break it down.

The Show: *"The Last Five Years* by Jason Robert Brown"

Before you even consider going to this call, you'd better learn a little about the play. I find that Amazon.com and iTunes are useful websites for the thrifty actor because they allow you to listen to snippets from the CD. You'll hear that this is a very contemporary, very poppy, and very complex score. I would also try to find the libretto (or at least portions of it) online to get a sense of who these characters are—again, Google is your friend.

The Theatre: "Pawtucket Players"

According to the ad, this is an established (30 yrs.) theatre. Visit their website, look at pictures, read reviews, and see who else has worked there. You should get an idea if this is the type of place you'd like to work before you go to the auditions.

The Staff: "Bill Jones, dir.; Sadie Hawkings, mus. dir."

This information can be helpful, particularly if you know or have some connections to the names listed. If you studied with Sadie's best pal when you were in college, make sure that name is prominently displayed on your résumé. Also, if you know people who have worked with Bill Jones, see what you can find out about him. Perhaps your friend has done several shows with Mr. Jones and tells you that the man *hates* Andrew Lloyd Webber's musicals. This would be a good indication that "Think of Me" from *The Phantom of the Opera* might not be your best audition selection this time around.

The Commitment: "Rehearsals begin July 1; Performances run from July 22 through August 13"

Are you available during this time span? If you're likely to have *any* conflicts during those six weeks, you'll want to mention them at the audition so that there are no surprises later on. I like actors to be up front with me about any unavailable times and dates at the initial audition. Having other commitments will not preclude you from being cast; rather, it will allow me to consider if I can feasibly use you in a particular role knowing that you won't be around for certain rehearsals. I recently did a production of *Cabaret*, and my first choice for the role of the Emcee was going to miss an entire week of rehearsals. This was a college production, so we were on a generous schedule, and I decided that this actor was worth the risk incurred with losing him for five rehearsals. It also gave his understudy the chance to get some work in and to hone his chops a bit. The actor I cast was very successful as the Emcee, and the time missed did not affect his work.

In some cases, it might not work out that well for an actor with other obligations, but it's always better to be up front with a director. You risk burning a bridge if you take the approach of "I'll just audition now, get the job, and spring this bit on him later." Too many actors have done that to me, and I'll never cast them again.

The Compensation: "$350/week plus housing"

Often negotiating is a possibility. More on that later. It is best, however, to assume for the time being that their price is final. Is this enough for you to take that six-week commitment? If the auditors are up front with you about how much they're offering, it's only fair that you will take this factor into consideration *before* you go in. If you absolutely can't work for that amount, *don't audition*. Sometimes there will be no pay at all—especially for small theatres around New York and Chicago, where actors just work for the exposure and the résumé credits. If you can't work for free, then *don't audition*. Many people will tell you that you should audition for everything, even if you can't or won't take the job. I must strongly advise against this theory. Remember, the director is trying in earnest to cast her production. Your coming in for exposure or for practice and subsequently rejecting a job offer may be seen by that director as a waste of her valuable time. You may burn a bridge this way as well.

The Audition: "Friday, June 29, and Saturday, June 30, from 12 p.m. to 3 p.m. at the Pawtucket High School auditorium"

There is no indication on this call that you need an appointment, so just show up. Often, you will need to submit a picture and résumé in advance to schedule an audition time. For those calls, you'll need to draft a cover letter—we'll discuss cover letters and mailings in a later chapter. For this audition, however, simply get there and plan to arrive early. I'm a firm believer in "the earlier, the better." If you show up at 11:30 a.m. on Friday to sign up, it tells me that you're eager to work and that you're punctual. It also allows you to set the bar against which every actor who follows you will have to compete. Waiting until the end (while it won't keep you from being cast by any means) may show a lack of interest on your part. The role may already be well decided by the end of auditions. And quite frankly, the director's attention span may be too exhausted for you to have every advantage in your audition. Come early. If given the opportunity, go first. Trust me, it counts for something!

Variations on a Theme

Remember to read the audition notice carefully. The majority of auditions will either be open calls of the same nature as my example or auditions by appointment, for which you will need to mail in a headshot, résumé, and cover letter and await a call from the producers or the director. However, there are always other variables that may come into play depending on the nature of the particular show being cast:

1. They might be "typing out." Often at open cattle calls, if the crowd is too large to see everyone, the casting director may decide to type out before he hears people. This means they literally line people up in groups and they look at everyone and choose people to stay and audition based purely on look and type. Or they may call everyone in and dismiss anyone who has less than 10 years of tap experience. Whatever you do, don't take this personally!

2. They may have separate calls for "dancers who sing" and "actors who move." Be sure to attend the audition that is most suited to your skills—if you're not an incredible dancer, do not attend the dance audition when you have the option to do a "singers who move" audition. Typically, the dance combination will be much faster and more complex at the dancer call.

3. They may only be seeking actors for specific roles. If you see a character breakdown, be sure to pay attention to which parts are open. Do not submit yourself for or gear your audition toward a role that has already been cast.

The Requirements: "Two contrasting 16-bar cuttings from contemporary musical theatre"

Here again, a working knowledge of the show will really be an advantage to you. Besides the fact that our fictional friend Bill Jones hates Lloyd Webber, one listen to the score of *The Last Five Years* will tell you that "Think of Me" is not appropriate for the role of Cathy. You want to try to find audition pieces that allow directors to see who you are and what you can do, while also capturing the essence of the character for which you're auditioning.

I personally have no problem with actors auditioning with music from the show itself—sometimes I even encourage it. How better to determine your appropriateness for Jamie than to hear you handle his songs from the show. Some instructors, however, disagree with this approach. They feel as though singing "Maria" for a *West Side Story* audition would somehow pigeonhole you out of consideration for the role of Riff. I think this is utter nonsense—give directors some credit for imagination! Besides, if you sing for Tony but I see you as Riff, I can always use the callback to test you in that role.

And yet, a quirk such as "no singing from the show" is just another reason that knowing who's directing can be an advantage to you as a smart actor. *Flom's directing it? Great! He'll love it if I sing "Shiksa Goddess!"*

One solution to the contentious issue of pulling material from the show they're casting is to use a song by the same composer. Look at what else Brown wrote and find music that has a similar style—that captures the *essence* of the show you're going in for. When you walk in the door, you can always ask the director if he minds hearing selections from the show, and if the response is yes, you'll have a suitable Plan B.

Note: this ad calls for 16 bars, or measures, of music. Remember, *never* go into an audition knowing *only* 16 bars or any shortened version of your song. You must be prepared to sing the entire song if they ask you to. You'd be surprised how often directors will be dazzled with your voice and want to hear more—or disappointed that you cut a song the way you did and want to hear a different, more revealing portion (e.g., "Can you jump to the bridge?" or "Let's hear how you handle the modulation in the last verse"). In these situations, you don't want to tell them you learned only your 16-bar cutting. It's unprofessional and counterproductive, not to mention embarrassing. To that end, avoid coming to auditions with an anthology of 16-bar audition cuttings. These are actually becoming very popular publications for their ease of use. Don't be lazy; learn the whole song. Nail it. Then choose *your best* 16 bars to show them at the audition. Finally on the subject of cutting, remember this simple axiom: Always leave 'em wanting more. Even if a casting call says to prepare two songs, there's no rule that says you have to sing the songs in their entirety. If you know that your song is repetitive and that you can show them everything they need to see in a verse and a chorus, then by all means *do it*. Less is more. Even generous directors who afford actors the opportunity to do a full-song audition get restless once they've seen what they need to see. Sometimes a great singer who saves the "good stuff" for the end has already lost his audience after the first uneventful two minutes. I know directors who will even cut actors off midsong once they have either heard or not heard what they are looking for. If you can show them what they need (namely, your "money" notes and your acting chops) in a fraction of the time, they'll love you for it. And remember, if they want to hear more, they'll ask you to sing more: advantage, you. After all, that's what callbacks are for, and your job at an audition is to *get a callback*.

The Open Roles: "Seeking: Jamie—male; 26-30 . . . Cathy—female; 23-28 . . ."

Pay attention to this. Some ads won't list sought roles at all (one may safely assume that all roles then would be open), but if they do list characters, you must read carefully. The descriptions given are a summary of how this theatre describes the characters it is casting. They may very well contain interpreted choices, and so it would behoove you to be clear on what they're looking for.

I directed a production of *Forever Plaid* some years ago, and I cast out of New York City. Although I'm generally a big advocate of cross-gender and non-traditional casting choices, I was taking a very classic approach to this production, and so my casting breakdown specified: Four men, early- to mid-20s. I was shocked at the number of women who sent me headshots and very generic cover letters. I normally keep interesting submissions even if a person is wrong for the current project—I'll look back through my files and call on them later when something more appropriate arises. However, I tossed away every female submission for *Plaid* simply because I felt they showed a lack of concern and understanding for what they were applying for. Granted, this may sound grumpy and overreactive on my part, but when you consider that I was receiving 60 to 100 envelopes each day before this audition, I resented what I considered a waste of my time (ah, the young arrogant director!). I'm sure that not all directors would react this way, but why not just avoid the possibility and save the postage and the headshot while you're at it? Concentrate on finding the shows that you are right for.

And remember, this is show *business*, not show amusement or show pastime. The people casting have a business to run, and time is money. If they perceive you as wasting their time, they are less likely to want to hire you for current or future projects. You need to treat all of your work like it's a business. People in the industry will respect you much more.

The Union Affiliations: "Equity/Non-Equity Performers"

Take this information with a grain of salt. If a call is listed as a nonunion gig, then there's generally no flexibility to allow for a (rule-abiding) Equity member to be cast. However, just because a show is a union production does not negate nonunion folks from consideration. Many of my friends were cast in their first Broadway productions before becoming members of Actors' Equity. In fact, now that the old points system is becoming more and more outmoded, it seems that the clearest way to gain access into the union is in fact to be cast in your first Equity show. In a later chapter, I'll address the union issue in more detail, but for now, just be aware that it is possible to "crash" an Equity call if you don't have your card. This usually involves lining up at excruciatingly early hours and waiting all day in the hopes that they'll have time at the end to see you. But if it's worth the day to be seen by this particular director or this particular theatre, then why not go for it?

If you decide to go in for an Equity call, you'll need to arrive an hour or two before the posted sign-in time. Usually there will be a line-up, so being early is necessary for nonunion members. When they begin to sign people in, you will be put on a list and given a tentative time to return—usually late in the afternoon. If the director finishes seeing all of the Equity performers before the day is through, she may at her own discretion spend some time seeing non-Equity actors as well. Even if it's a long shot to get cast, these calls are often a good opportunity for some early exposure to big casting directors. I believe it's worth it to attend them at least once or twice in a while.

Before You Walk Out that Door . . .

So here you are: an actor. You've been taking classes; you're confident (or at least you're prepared to *act* confident); you've got a decent headshot, a growing, well-organized repertoire book, and a subscription to a trade paper or website. You've read up on some good auditions coming up. What else must you do before you head into the studios to dazzle the director? Just a couple of things. . . .

First, be prepared for *anything*. When you see someone trudging down a city street with a giant duffle bag, carrying what seems to be his whole life on his shoulder, before you assume he's homeless, consider that he's very likely an actor. An actor must dress comfortably enough to navigate the city in any weather, but at the same time, he must be prepared to look his best in an audition after running 16 blocks on his lunch break to be seen for *The Full Monty*. There are conflicting notions on whether or not you should "dress the role" you're going in for. I think this really depends, and I leave it to your best judgment to make that call for yourself. For example, you wouldn't want to wear a suit to an audition for *Hair*, a laid-back, counterculture rock musical; but you also don't need to dress like a vagabond if you're being seen for the Homeless Woman in *A New Brain*. I generally suggest a good casual-yet-professional audition outfit that allows you to feel confident that you look great at any given audition. The bottom line is, if they need to see you in a certain look, they'll ask you to adjust your outfit at the callbacks.

At musical auditions, they may ask you to stay and dance, so you'll want to have some dance clothes to change into. You'll need your music book as well as *at least ten* copies of your headshot/résumé. You should *always* have your headshot with you—even when not going to an audition. You never know when you might meet a potential employer. You'll need water and probably a snack in case it's a long day of auditions, and many people also choose to bring a book or some work to do to pass the time.

If that hasn't all weighed you down, consider that many actors carry changes of clothing and/or shoes just in case the audition turns out that it does indeed require a different aesthetic. (*This director isn't even consider-*

ing men under 5'7" . . . good thing you brought your boots!). Or in the frequent event that while attending one audition, you'll stumble onto another prime casting opportunity at the same studio. Better to be prepared than to be caught off-guard. Now, aren't you glad you divided your music into your huge collection "B" book, which is resting comfortably on your desk at home, and your easy-to-tote "A" book, which is not causing a curvature of your spine?

I must reiterate that it's incumbent upon you to *be prepared* in every possible way. I know this is a broad statement, and it's essentially the point of this entire book, but I will be very specific here for a moment.

An actor's job is to take care of the voice, take care of the body, and learn the lines. Before an audition, you *must* give yourself enough time to attend to your voice and body and have them in optimum readiness. For some, this might take two hours and a steaming for the sinuses; for others, some brief vocal scales and a good reach to the sky and toe-touch will do. You need to learn how your personal instrument operates and prepare accordingly to be in prime condition when you walk into the room. Attending auditions frequently is one way of conditioning the body and voice to be ready always.

A full vocal and physical warm-up is ideal, but in reality it's not always possible. At the very least, be sure you do plenty of speaking in various vocal registers throughout the hours leading up to an audition. This will get you minimally opened up. If you're in a car, sing along with the radio. If you're in a place where you have some room to move, stretch your body out before heading to the audition. Once you get in the room, you only have about 30 to 60 seconds to impress the artistic staff, so you don't have time to "warm into" your audition as you go. Be at performance level when you walk in the room so you don't shoot yourself in the foot before they get the chance to see how great you are.

Often when you arrive at the audition site, there will be a holding room where performers can stretch and vocalize, but you shouldn't bank on this. Furthermore, be sure you *arrive early* to your audition appointment. You'll want some time to focus and breathe a little before you face the auditors. They may even be running early (if it happens to be the second Monday after the third full moon of the second rain of the season with Venus rising . . .), and you don't want to keep them waiting. Technically, if you have an appointed time and the auditions are running fast, they must give you the option of waiting until your scheduled slot. But think of how they'll appreciate your willingness to move things along and to keep them ahead of schedule! Just another way of making yourself look professional.

Remember the old theatre adage: If you're 15 minutes early, you're on time; if you're on time, you're late.

Be on time. Be prepared. Be happy to perform.

SUMMARY

- No director wants actors to fail in the audition. He is hoping for you to be exactly what the role requires. He is also looking for actors who are tenacious, enthusiastic, and professional.
- Act everything. Do not simply sing pretty and dance well and save your acting choices for the monologue. Act the song and dance.
- Take classes and continue to study as often as you can.
- Do not rely on monologue books, film, or the Internet for source material. Read and see plays for age-appropriate pieces.
- Learn music from the notations on the page, not from the cast recording.
- Know every song in your "A" repertoire book by rote.
- Be sure to have at least one contemporary and one standard ballad and up-tempo song in your book that you can pull out for any audition.
- Photocopy your music and organize it neatly, in non-glare sheets, in a binder. Do not bring loose pages or vocal selection books.
- Be prepared to sing anything in your book, as well as songs from any shows listed on your résumé.
- Be sure to read and understand casting call ads thoroughly before responding or attending an audition.
- Look for appropriate audition material for the specific show you're going in for; consider songs from the same composer or genre, or songs that convey the essence of the role you are interested in.
- Never learn only 16 bars of a song. Be prepared to sing the entire piece if asked.
- Be prepared for anything at an audition!
- Always carry copies of your headshot and résumé with you wherever you go.

2

A DETAILED GUIDE TO BUILDING THE ACTOR'S REPERTOIRE BOOK

The repertoire book is the most important tool in a musical theatre performer's arsenal. The contents of your book must tell a director who you are and what you can do. It should be diverse and varied, showcasing you at your best in a wide variety of different genres and styles. It is important to remember that no matter what stage of your career you find yourself in, the rep book is an ongoing, ever-growing project. It changes as you mature, learn new songs, learn new styles, discover exciting new material, and so forth. So whether you are just starting out and are new to this whole repertoire thing, or you are a seasoned pro with an enormous collection of songs and monologues, this section has some tips for success to create the best possible rep book, one you can bring into auditions with confidence.

I am going to walk you through a detailed process starting at the very beginning. By the end of this section, you should have a good working knowledge of how to keep your book in order for an entire career in this business. If you already have a book together and you're thinking of skipping over or skimming this section, I would advise you instead to read on. When I work with my students on repertoire, I make them pull everything out of their books and start from scratch. They inevitably find that following this method leads them to a much more organized, polished, stronger set of repertoire than they had before. So indulge me and be brave. Starting from zero again can be scary, but you'll be better off for it in the end.

STEP 1: GATHER THE NECESSARY EQUIPMENT

You will need to obtain *two* sturdy three-ring binders. The first one should be 1½ to 2½ inches thick. Any thicker would be too large and any thinner won't hold enough music. You may want the second binder to be larger, as this will house the bulk of your music that you are not toting around to every audition; this is your "B" book.

You will also need a large quantity of clear plastic *nonglare* sheets to protect your music. It is important that the package say "nonglare"; otherwise, your accompanist may have a hard time seeing the notes on the page if the light in the audition room is bad.

Other materials you may want to have handy are tab dividers (if you wish to separate your binder into individual songs or sections), a black marker, and a yellow highlighter. Now you have everything you need to begin building the rep book.

STEP 2: SEARCH FOR MATERIAL

When I told you to start from scratch no matter where you are in your career, I did not mean to imply that you needed to find all new material. In fact, the best place to begin to find material is among the songs that you already know. If you have music in vocal scores, vocal selection books, or variety collections (e.g., the Soprano's Musical Theatre Songbook), you will need to begin by copying the music onto loose sheets. Copying the songs may seem redundant if you already own the music books, but trust me: you do not want a pianist trying to play for you out of a vocal selections book. The pages never stay open and it can be the downfall of your audition. It is not the professional way to deliver your songs to the accompanist.

If you do not own any collections already, you can generally find them at any major book store. If you are seeking a specific musical, I would suggest checking online at www.amazon.com, www.dramabookshop.com, or www .colonymusic.com. A good public library is a terrific source for finding sheet music when you don't want to pay for an entire book. Simply find the scores section, check out the shows you are interested in, and copy the individual song(s) you need. Just be sure when you copy music out of a book that you get the entire page copied clearly onto your paper. If the score is oversized, as many original vocal scores are, you may need to reduce the size on the copy machine; reduction to 93% generally works perfectly. Do be sure that none of the lyrics, notes, or dynamic markings are cut off. Sometimes when copying out of a large book you will find that the staff ends up slanted across the printed page. It's best if you try to make the music straight. And if the title of the song does not fit, be sure to write it in.

One other valuable source for finding sheet music is the Internet. There are websites that allow you to buy individual songs for a nominal fee and print them out right on your home computer. The best of these that I have found is www.musicnotes.com, which not only sells songs but also lets the buyer transpose the music into different keys if the original is too high or too low. I would beware this luxury, as many musical directors will expect to hear songs in their original key—especially classic musical theatre tunes. But occasionally, this function can be appropriate and helpful.

So now that you know where to look for music, let's spend some time talking about what music to look for. As I mentioned before, it is vital that you have music representing a variety of styles, eras, and genres. It is not enough anymore to rely on old standards by George and Ira Gershwin or Richard Rodgers and Oscar Hammerstein II to get you through every audition. Often nowadays, musicals are based on rock, country, or even hip-hop idioms, and frequently actors will be asked specifically not to sing songs from musical theatre. And so you must, as a smart musical theatre actor, be very hip to current trends. You must see and listen to a lot of musicals as well as a variety of popular music. For example, country music may not be your favorite style, but shows like *Spitfire Grill*, *Pump Boys and Dinettes*, and *Floyd Collins* are produced with enough regularity that it would help to know something about that singing style. I recommend that all young, handsome men give a listen to artists like Frank Sinatra, Dean Martin, Sammy Davis Jr., Tony Bennett, and the likes to learn how to croon. This is also a style that never goes out of vogue.

In the back of this book there is an appendix with a checklist of genres. You can use it for easy reference later on, but for now I'll be more detailed. Also, please realize that my suggestions all come with the caveat that you must be able to perform each of these types of songs well before adding them to your repertoire—it does you no good to have operetta in your book, for example, if you cannot sing it; rather, I would advise you to either learn how to handle those songs or avoid operetta auditions if it isn't your thing. And that goes for any genre that you don't feel at home performing. You should love to sing every song in your book. If you don't enjoy it, take it out.

I can now segue perfectly into the discussion on material with the first type (in chronological order) of music to include in a complete book: operetta. If you are classically trained or have the ability to shift into this mode, it is not a bad idea to have a song that showcases your legit voice in the operatic fashion. Many stock and regional theatres will include Gilbert and Sullivan in their seasons (most commonly, *The Mikado*, *The Pirates of Penzance*, and *H.M.S. Pinafore*). If they are interested in casting you for a summer company, they may require that you handle classical singing as well as contemporary musical theatre. Also, there are several reputable companies in New York that produce these works annually, including the Gilbert and Sullivan Players and the Village Light Opera Group. Again, if you can do it, it might be another avenue toward a career in performing. Operetta, however, may be one of the genres that you only need to add to your "A" book on days when you know you are going to audition for a theatre that does operetta. Use your best judgment on that.

Songs from the aforementioned Gilbert and Sullivan works will suffice in your book. For girls, consider an aria such as "The Sun Whose Rays" from *The Mikado* or "Poor Wand'ring One" from *The Pirates of Penzance*. For men, you may want a patter song (tour de force of words, very common in operetta), such as "I am the Very Model of a Modern Major General" from *Penzance*. These examples are very common and somewhat cliché in the world of operetta, but for a musical theatre performer to have something simple to pull out, they should be fine. Consider searching deeper, however, and looking into the works of Rudolf Friml, Sigmund Romberg, and Victor Herbert if this style suits your voice and your ambitions. Also a note for African American performers: *Porgy and Bess* by Gershwin contains some of the most beautiful opera music intended to be sung by actors of color. If you do not know this show, you should.

Next, you will need ballad and up-tempo representation from what we call jazz standards. This music may have been written specifically for the theatre or film (such as much of the work of Harold Arlen), or it may have been used in various musicals not originally intended for the song (such as much of the Gershwins' work). It may even be from the popular catalog, not associated with the theatre at all. The bulk of this music will come from the 1920s, '30s, and '40s, but you can even find good jazz standards being written today and performed by the likes of Harry Connick Jr. and Michael Bublé. This genre includes music that is meant to be crooned like Sinatra or Bobby Darin; it also includes sultry torch songs and swing music as performed by Ella Fitzgerald and Billie Holiday.

In the category of jazz standards, many of the stipulations that will apply to choosing songs from later musical theatre, such as age, gender, and race appropriateness, need not usually be a concern. In other words, both men and women should consider singing a tune like "Orange Colored Sky" by Milton DeLugg and Willie Stein or "It's Only a Paper Moon" by Harold

Arlen, E. Y. Harburg, and Billy Rose. This style also leaves a great amount of room for interpretation; hence, you will rarely find a song sounding the same in different recordings by multiple jazz artists. It is vital, however, that you first learn the music exactly as it is printed on the page before you attempt to style the song. And do not simply listen to someone else's rendition of the song and think that you should (or could) sing it like him or her. I had a student who in our lesson attempted to sing some tunes by Michael Bublé. He was completely thrown when the piano accompaniment sounded nothing like the big band on the CD he had been practicing with at home. That student scrapped those song options because he couldn't separate the song from the singer.

Closely associated with jazz standards is a category I call pre–Golden Age musical theatre. This includes music that was written specifically for the stage and appeared in musicals dating before the early 1940s—the era now known as the Golden Age of Musicals (more on that soon). Often these musicals produced what are now considered jazz standards, but occasionally there were divergences. The pre–Golden Age genre includes the works of Richard Rodgers and Lorenz Hart (*Pal Joey, Babes in Arms*), George and Ira Gershwin (*Oh, Kay!, Girl Crazy*), and Kurt Weill (*The Threepenny Opera, Lady in the Dark, One Touch of Venus*). It also includes the frequently produced flapper-style musicals, such as *Good News!* and *No, No, Nanette*.

This era is distinguished by a songwriting style that can be labeled "vertical." Vertical songs are those that neither further the plot along nor develop character—hence, they are vertical on a time line of the story. These are songs that can be (and often are) lifted from one show and used in another; they are not written for any specific character. In fact, it was not uncommon in the '20s and '30s for composers to have a bevy of music that they had written as stand-alone songs, and they would insert whatever song sounded appropriate in the given plot when the need arose. One small detail that sometimes distinguishes jazz standards from pre–Golden Age music is that the pre–Golden Age songs are usually, at the very least, gender specific—though not always.

It is sufficient to have one or two ballads and one or two up-tempos from the '20s through the early '40s. Again, you can work on a wider array of songs, but you can leave most of them in your "B" book and just take along the really hot ones with you on a daily basis. If you want a great way of finding appropriate music from this era, simply grab yourself some "songbook" CDs, such as Ella Fitzgerald sings Rodgers and Hart or Frank Sinatra sings Gershwin, for example. One further note to African American singers: *Ain't*

Misbehavin' by Fats Waller contains some of the greatest jazz-age music ever written. Like *Porgy*, it is meant to be performed by actors of color, so you may look there for some exciting material as well.

It is also important to point out that although many of these genres are associated with a particular decade or era, it is often appropriate to find music of a similar style from a different time period to answer an audition call. For instance, "Sooner or Later" from the movie musical *Dick Tracy* (1990, music by Stephen Sondheim) or any number of songs from the musical *City of Angels* (1989, Cy Coleman, David Zippel, and Larry Gelbart) would be good choices for a jazz-era musical. Similarly, songs from *Thoroughly Modern Millie* (2002, Jeanine Tesori, Dick Scanlan, and Richard Morris) or *The Boy Friend* (1954, Sandy Wilson) would be perfect for an audition for the flapper musicals of the 1920s, as they are set in the same period and modeled after those musicals.

The next genre is commonly known in the musical theatre world as the Golden Age. This is perhaps the most vast and most popular period of musicals. The Golden Age begins with *Oklahoma!* (1943, Richard Rodgers and Oscar Hammerstein II) and runs up through *Fiddler on the Roof* (1964, Jerry Bock and Sheldon Harnick). It is characterized by musicals in which the book, songs, and dance were fully integrated. In other words, characters did not stop the plot to sing or dance; rather, the songs and dances carried the story further. Thus, the music of the Golden Age is mostly "horizontal" in nature. These musicals all bear striking similarity in structure. There was a formula for the placement of large production numbers, duets, comedy songs, and so forth, that seemed to prove very successful with audiences of the day. That formula is still effective today, although many contemporary composers have found fortune in working against the accepted norm of the Golden Age.

You cannot be a complete musical theatre performer if you do not have songs from this genre in your book. It may actually be the most valuable, versatile music you can find. I usually recommend to my students that they have a couple of ballads and a couple of up-tempos from this genre—at least one of which should be by Rodgers and Hammerstein.

In the Golden Age you must begin to concern yourself with a character's age, gender, and race when choosing songs. While it is usually acceptable in today's society of color-blind and nontraditional casting for minority ethnicities to sing from nearly any role, it is not general practice for Caucasians to sing roles specifically written for Blacks or Asians, for example. There are exceptions to this rule (often including material from *The Wiz* and *Once on This Island*), but those exceptions are subject to the sensibilities of a particular director. So it's important to be careful when singing race-specific material; know who you are going in to audition for.

This is your opportunity to really seek out roles in which you would be dynamite. Do not be afraid to use music from familiar shows, as most of the musicals of this time period are well known. You will never be able to reinvent the wheel and sing something from the Golden Age that they've never heard (If they've never heard it, there's probably a good reason!), so just find some songs that are not too cliché and perform them very well.

Shows to consider include *South Pacific, Me and Juliet,* and *State Fair* by Richard Rodgers and Oscar Hammerstein II; *Brigadoon* by Alan J. Lerner and Frederick Loewe; *How to Succeed in Business without Really Trying* by Frank Loesser; *On the Town* and *Wonderful Town* by Leonard Bernstein with Betty Comden and Adolph Green; *Bells are Ringing* by Jule (pronounced Julie!) Styne with Comden and Green; *Kiss Me, Kate* by Cole Porter; *She Loves Me* and *Fiddler on the Roof* by Bock and Harnick; and *Damn Yankees* and *The Pajama Game* by Richard Adler and Jerry Ross. The list could go on forever, but I'll save that for another book. Just know that you have a myriad of choices, so seek out the songs that fit well in your voice and showcase your acting. And do not sing songs that are well out of your age range. If you are in high school, you don't necessarily have to find characters who are in high school as well, but you certainly shouldn't be singing mother- and father-age roles.

Again moving chronologically, our next period would be the popular movements of the 1950s and '60s. Many shows are either set in or take their cue from the introduction of the rock and roll idiom into pop music of this time. Musicals such as *Grease, Bye Bye Birdie, Smokey Joe's Café,* and more recently *Jersey Boys* call upon a performer's ability to sing in the style made popular by Elvis Presley, Buddy Holly, and Frankie Valli. Furthermore, if cruise ships and theme parks interest you as a venue for performing, you'll need a 1950s song for almost any of their auditions. These songs may be from shows set in the period, or you may choose to pull from the popular music catalog. Songs to look at include "Runaway" by Del Shannon, "Dancing in the Street" performed by Martha and the Vandellas, "Oh, Boy" by Buddy Holly, "Ruby Baby" by Jerry Leiber and Mike Stoller, "One Night with You" by Elvis Presley, and "Since I Don't Have You" by the Skyliners. This list can go on forever as well. Just find a song or two that you sing well that also sounds great being played on a piano.

The next category to look into is 1960s and '70s musical theatre. These composers aren't quite pop or rock writers, although that music began to be popular in the same time period. Rather, these are the artists who continued in the Golden Age tradition and wrote mainly what are considered "show tunes" for the stage. I am speaking of Jerry Herman, John Kander and Fred Ebb, Tom Jones and Harvey Schmidt, Cy Coleman, and the like. Last year we brought multiple teams of agents and casting directors out to look at our seniors at Shenandoah Conservatory. Despite the students' best efforts to find edgy, unusual, off-beat material, all of the NY Theatre professionals would inevitably ask the student for either a standard, a Golden Age song, or a piece by Kander and Ebb. You cannot underestimate the value of these genres in your repertoire. Go figure.

Modern pop and rock music began to find their way into the world of theatre back in the 1960s, and they continue to pervade Broadway scores even today. I divide them into two separate genres: musical theatre pop and musical theatre rock, and I suggest you look for representative songs from both styles.

Musical theatre pop includes the work of Stephen Schwartz, William Finn, Richard Maltby and David Shire, Craig Carnelia, and Lynn Ahrens and Stephen Flaherty, to name a few. These are artists who were clearly influenced by light rock of their time, but the music is specific to character and plot.

Musical theatre rock scores include *Hair*, *The Who's Tommy*, *Bat Boy: The Musical*, *Spring Awakening*, and *The Rocky Horror Show*. Like the musical theatre pop category, these composers are influenced by popular rock music, but the songs are show- and character-specific. You may choose to have a selection from these musicals, or you may simply have one or two actual pop-rock songs. Quite often, audition calls for rock shows will specify that they do not wish to hear theatre music.

It is important that whatever songs you choose for this category sound good played on a piano, since most rock music is guitar and percussion driven. Rock artists whose work tends to lend itself well to auditions include Billy Joel, Elton John, Meat Loaf, The Beatles, Elvis Presley, Linda Ronstadt, Journey, Heart, Pat Benatar, The Who, and Queen. I would suggest that before taking a rock song into an audition you have it played on a piano for you so that you can hear how it sounds without any guitars or drums. If you feel like you can still use that song in the way you intended, then go with it. If, however, it is too jarring to lose all of the electricity of the original recording, then find another choice.

When you attempt to perform this music, it should not sound like musical theatre singing. Directors who take on rock operas or jukebox musicals are looking for singers who can "rock out" and style the songs. So however you handle this music when you're alone in your car with the windows down and the radio blasting or when you're singing in the shower is how you should deliver in an audition. Don't try to act out the specific lyrics to these songs; you'll just look foolish. Rather, just identify an overarching mood or singular objective and commit fully to that throughout the performance of the song.

I already mentioned country music as a common genre in the theatre today. Like rock, you may want to have a legitimate country song rather than a theatre song. I suggest listening to artists like Dolly Parton, Dixie Chicks, Patsy Cline, Johnny Cash, Willie Nelson, Waylon Jennings, and Emmylou Harris. As with the approach to rock music, you need to sell the mood and the style with country, not necessarily the acting choices.

Those nine categories compose a pretty comprehensive repertoire for the beginner or even the professional performer. If you have selections from operetta, jazz standards, pre-Golden Age, Golden Age, the '50s, '60s, and '70s show tunes, pop, rock, and country, there isn't an audition for which you shouldn't have suitable material. However, there are some other things you may want to consider having in your "B" book, ready to go when the situation calls for it.

Stephen Sondheim gets his own category. Many in the theatre consider Sondheim to be the greatest composer/lyricist the stage has ever seen. His music and lyrics are nearly inseparable from the characters who sing them, and he is a genius wordsmith. His music is also incredibly complicated to sing and to play. There's an old adage in the theatre that says "never sing Sondheim at an audition." This is only mostly true. The reason has mainly to do with the complexity of the accompaniment. Yet, there are times when a Sondheim piece would be appropriate—especially if you know the accompanist can handle it. One such occasion is when you are auditioning for a Sondheim show.

Some of his songs to look at for auditions include "What More Do I Need?" from *Saturday Night*; "I Remember" from *Evening Primrose*; "That'll Show Him" and "Lovely" from *A Funny Thing Happened on the Way to the Forum*; "Good Thing Going" and "Not a Day Goes By" from *Merrily We Roll Along*; and "Unworthy of Your Love" from *Assassins*. Be careful to avoid some of his challenging patter songs such as "Franklin Shepherd, Inc." and "Buddy's Blues." And also be careful not to sing some of his wonderful songs written for older characters but frequently misplaced in young actors' repertoires, such as "Send in the Clowns," "Broadway Baby," and "Ladies Who Lunch."

It's also not a bad idea to have something from current Broadway offerings just to show that you are keeping up with the latest trends. And you may want to find an obscure song or two that no one else is singing regularly—this can become a conversation piece in the audition room and pique their interest if the mood is right. In fact, if you really want to be a risk taker you can think outside the box and consider a specialty song that nobody is doing that shows off your voice as well as your sense of humor. I have been sworn to secrecy as to the identity of the song, but I can tell you that I have a friend who has worked nonstop by auditioning with a theme song from an old television show. As long as the auditors are from the generation when that show was popular, they always have a laugh and comment on how much they enjoyed the selection. Sometimes being risky pays off!

Speaking of obscure songs, I want to reiterate what I said before about the agents and casting directors asking my students to sing standards and Golden Age music. Many performers find it necessary to dig deep into the catalog of lost, unproduced, and forgotten musicals to find songs that no one has heard. They are so concerned with singing what nobody else is singing, they lose track of good taste. While it is occasionally appropriate and beneficial to have songs that are really your own, it is far more helpful to have songs with which most directors are at least vaguely familiar. This way, they will have some standard against which to judge your rendition of the song. There is nothing wrong with singing a familiar melody, as long as you sing it well.

Of course, that being said, there are some tunes that are so familiar you may want to avoid them completely. Everyone has their own list of "do not sing" songs, so here are some of mine:

"Nothing" from *A Chorus Line*; Any songs from *The Phantom of the Opera* or *Les Miserables*; "This Is the Moment" from *Jekyll and Hyde*; "Oh, What a Beautiful Morning" from *Oklahoma!*; "Getting to Know You" from *The King and I*; "Gethsemane" from *Jesus Christ Superstar*; "Soliloquy" from *Carousel*; "Corner of the Sky" from *Pippin*; "Someone to Watch Over Me" from *Oh, Kay!*; "I Got Rhythm" from *Girl Crazy*; "Anything Goes" from *Anything Goes*; "Adelaide's Lament" from *Guys and Dolls*; "Just You Wait" from *My Fair Lady*; "My Favorite Things" from *The Sound of Music*; "Shy" from *Once Upon a Mattress*; "Vanilla Ice Cream" from *She Loves Me*; "Popular" and "Defying Gravity" from *Wicked*; and "All That Jazz" from *Chicago*. I'm sure there are more, but I try to block them from my mind. There is nothing wrong with any of these songs, per se, other than the fact that they are overdone in auditions.

Finally, some other songs to avoid include anything with dialect (*My Fair Lady*, Adelaide in *Guys and Dolls*, Audrey in *Little Shop of Horrors*), and any songs that either build you up enormously ("Gorgeous" from *The Apple*

Tree, "Astonishing" from *Little Women*; "The Greatest Star" from *Funny Girl*) or self-deprecate and make a statement that you are a loser ("Mr. Cellophane" from *Chicago*, "Nobody Does It Like Me" from *Seesaw* and "You Can Always Count on Me" from *City of Angels*). If you are attending an audition for any of those shows, then you may use those songs. Otherwise, leave them in your "B" book or on the cutting room floor.

STEP 3: LEARN THE SONGS

I am now going to offer you advice on how to approach every song you learn, with the exception of pop music, which has no dramatic context. You will likely read this section and scoff at the amount of work it requires of you, especially in light of the quantity of songs I just suggested for your repertoire. You may want to take shortcuts or perhaps avoid doing the work on songs you already "know." But I guarantee you that if you have not done this analysis, you do not truly know the songs you have been singing. When my students complain to me about how much time this requires, I tell them what my acting teacher Jim Wise always told us in graduate school: If this were easy, everyone would do it. Now begins the real work of the actor.

The first step to learning a song properly is to begin with the lyrics. If you have never heard the song, this step will be easier, as you will not have a preconceived rhythm or tune in your head. If you do know the tune, try your best to separate yourself from it and look at the words as an entity of their own. Begin by writing or typing out the lyrics in paragraph form, taking them out of verse and removing the composer's punctuation. This will allow you to read the song as a text without any poetic quirks. Next, add in the punctuation that makes sense, including periods, question marks, exclamation points, commas, colons, semi-colons, hyphens, and so forth. Then begin to learn the piece as a monologue, focusing only on the words and their meaning.

At this point I am assuming that you know the story line of the musical from which your song comes and you have thought about the character and the song's dramatic context. Look for red flags such as repeated lyrics, symbolism, metaphor, alliteration, and consonance to point out which words the lyricist felt were important in the conveyance of the song's meaning. Why are those techniques used, and how can you use them to make your performance more powerful? Circle the nouns and think about what they mean to your character so that when you speak and sing them, they come to life clearly. Then begin to consider why the character *needs* to sing this song (remember, in musical theatre characters sing when the emotion is too great to speak). What does he want from his scene partner? What kinds of tactics can he use to achieve his objective? Is there seduction, guilt, reasoning, pleading, bargaining? When you have thought through all of these questions thoroughly, you should begin to memorize your lyrics as a monologue and then practice delivering it as such. Use a mirror, or better yet, a scene partner, and speak the text aloud, paying close attention to words and phrases that need to be emphasized or driven home. And do not cheat: If there are repeated words or verses, you should find a justification for the repetition. Why do we repeat ourselves when we speak? Why do we *repeat* ourselves when we speak? Why. Do. We. Repeat. Ourselves. When. We. Speak? Get it?

Once you have made a full analysis of the lyrics, you are ready to begin looking at the music. Just as you found red flags in the words, I encourage you to do the same with the composition. Even if you don't read music, you can look for clues like high notes and low notes that stand out on the staff, dynamic markings and accents that tell you how loud or soft to sing or how to attack certain notes, and duration of notes (half notes, whole notes, held notes, fermatas, etc.). In good musical theatre composing, these are all indications of the mood or emotional life of the character, and you should use them. As a general rule of thumb, it is safe to assume that high notes and long notes have extra significance and meaning.

The next thing to look at is the accompaniment, or the music playing underneath what you are singing. If you can play piano, you should hammer this out before dealing with the melody line. Otherwise, have someone play it for you. Listen for clues such as tempo and symbolic underscoring. For example, in Sondheim's musical *Company*, there is a terrific song called "Another Hundred People." It deals with the overwhelming populous of New York City, and its accompaniment sounds very much like a train car plowing through. The accompaniment can tell you a lot about what kind of mood the composer is looking for. It is a big mistake to ignore clues in the piano line.

Finally, you are ready to plunk out the melody. Remember my warning about original cast recordings: if you rely on them to teach you the melody, you will surely be led astray. Learn the notes on the page perfectly before adding any styling or ornamentation.

Once you put all of this together, you should be ready to fully perform any song you choose to tackle. The analysis will help fuse the singing with the acting, and it will make the difference between a nice voice and a skilled musical theatre actor. Note the use of the term *actor*. It is not enough just to stand and sing. You must invest fully in the character's life of any song you perform, moment to moment. Anything less than this will not be competitive in this cutthroat business. For every song you sing, you should be able to answer the following questions: What show is it from? Who wrote the show? Which character is singing it? To whom is she singing? What does she want from that person? Trust me, these questions will come up in audition situations, and you do not want to be unprepared for them. So take the time before you even put a song in your "A" book to take it apart and learn it correctly.

STEP 4: CUT AND MARK YOUR MUSIC

Now that you know how to find music and learn it, the final element is to prepare it for the audition room. It is not enough to simply copy it all and place it in sheets. This is where your black marker and highlighter will come in handy.

First of all, you must have the entire song for every selection you choose to sing. The only exception to this rule is if you choose to sing a cutting from a duet in which your character sings an entire section that stands alone; in this case, you may cut out the other character (e.g., "No Other Love" from *Me and Juliet* or "People Will Say We're in Love" from *Oklahoma!*). Otherwise, I'm afraid it's not enough to learn only a small segment of any song. You never know when they'll want to hear more, and you'll be embarrassed if you are caught without all the music.

That said, for every song you sing, you must prepare a specific, stand-alone section, generally consisting of 16 measures (half a chorus) or 32 measures (whole chorus) of music. Rarely will auditions call for entire songs, so you want to be prepared to show them only what they are asking to see. Cutting songs is an art in itself, and there is no simple, generalized way to explain it. However, I will offer some guidelines.

First of all, do not simply assume that "16 bars" literally means 16 bars— that you should count out exactly 16 measures of music and sing only that much. Sixteen bars is an approximation that says they don't really want to hear more than a minute of singing. If you are singing a ballad or a slow-moving song, chances are you will find a cutting that is close to the actual measure count; but if you are singing an up-tempo, speedy song, you can usually get away with doubling the number of measures and it will feel like the same amount of song. The bottom line is, don't come in and sing an entire verse and a chorus. Just give them a snippet of the song so they can hear your voice and see you act.

You've probably heard some version of the cliché that the first impression is the most important. Keep this in mind when choosing a cutting of music. You don't want to start out too subtle and take three minutes to get to the "good stuff." You may not get a chance to get that far. So try to show them everything you need them to see in the first 30 seconds. This means that starting at the beginning of the song isn't usually the best idea. If anything, it is usually more productive to start at the song's end and count backwards until you come to the beginning of a logical phrase at approximately 16 bars (or however many the audition calls for).

Which brings me to logic. Please consider all the work you have done on lyric analysis. Make sure you are able to show them some acting in the songs you bring in to auditions. This means that the cuttings you choose must make sense and be complete thoughts. Nothing burns me more than when singers stop in the middle of a phrase because they reached the "limit." Don't leave us hanging on a thought!

So, as you consider where you are going to cut a song, you will want to mark clearly with the black marker a bracket around the beginning and the end and write "Start" and "Stop" in big, bold letters. Then you should highlight both of these markings to make them extra clear.

Other things to highlight in the music include the key signature (the sharps and flats at the beginning of a piece of music) and any changes of key that occur throughout the song, any dynamic markings that will affect the piano accompaniment, any repeats in the music that you are taking or ignoring, and any stylings you choose to observe, such as fermatas, extra rests, or caesuras (train tracks). These highlights will make the pianist take note in advance of elements that might otherwise cause a slowdown or a stoppage in the fluid accompaniment. They will make your performance as smooth as possible and you will audition with confidence.

Once you have made all the necessary markings in your music, you are ready to put it into protective sheets and add it to your binder. Be sure to line the pages up so that they require the fewest number of page turns possible. If you have an excerpt with an even number of pages, the first page of the excerpt should be a left page, so that two pages are visible at once. If the excerpt has an odd number of pages, the first page may be either on the left or right. And needless to say, a song with only two pages should be placed so that the pages face each other, rather than page one on the right side of the book and page two behind it. Use common sense when designing your book layout.

If you have songs that are fairly long, you may choose to display only the cutting of the song that you will most frequently use, placing the rest of the music behind the cutting in one plastic sheet. If asked for more of the song, you can then take it out from behind the cut pages and display it fairly quickly. Just be sure that if your cutting starts in the middle of a song, you write the title of the song, the show it comes from, and the key signature on the top of the first page of your cutting. Again, this is for the benefit of the accompanist.

When putting the music into your binder, it is completely a matter of preference how you organize the songs. Some may choose to lay out music by genres, as I demonstrated for you earlier. Others may separate ballads from up-tempos or organize chronologically. Whatever works for you is fine; there is no prescribed method. But you may wish to use tab dividers for ease of finding music quickly. Some performers even place a table of contents at the front of the book so they do not need to thumb through to see the titles they have. My only advice is that you place whatever song(s) you are going to sing at an audition in the front of the book for that particular audition. This will make the pianist's life easier and they will love you for it.

Once again, remember that the repertoire book is an ever-changing beast. It can change over the years as you outgrow songs you've been using or grow into songs you've wanted to use. It can change depending on the nature of the audition that you are planning to attend. It can even change based on your knowledge of the director and his or her preferences (Remember: never sing Lloyd Webber for Flom!). If you take care in building your rep book, it will serve you well for years, and you will always look professional, confident, and polished. Directors will want to work with you.

STEP 5: NOT SO FAST . . . YOU NEED MONOLOGUES!

One of the biggest challenges for my students seems to be finding good monologues. I'm not sure if it's because they really don't know where to look or if it's because they don't think that musical theatre performers need them. Maybe it's laziness. Either way, I have news for you: You need them if you are to call yourself an actor. Almost nothing will make you look less professional in an audition setting than being asked for a monologue and saying you don't have one prepared. There is simply no excuse for such personal mismanagement. So here are some tips for finding at least a modest selection of pieces:

Like musical repertoire, you want monologues that stem from different genres of theatre (*not* film, TV, or the Internet!). You need a mix of light, comedic pieces (not stand-up routines) and more dramatic pieces (not suicidal or utterly miserable). Furthermore, you need representation of classical and contemporary theatre.

Begin with Shakespeare. He is the master of dramatic literature, and he is the most commonly produced playwright even today. Avoid plays like *Macbeth, Hamlet,* and *Romeo and Juliet.* These are really too overdone. Instead, look to plays such as *Measure for Measure, Twelfth Night, King Lear, Taming of the Shrew, Much Ado about Nothing,* and *Cymbeline,* for starters. Shakespeare has a wealth of characters who are in their 20s or early 30s, so seek them out. And when looking for good material, do not limit yourself to scanning the book for long paragraphs. Often the best monologues come from taking a scene of dialogue and cutting the minor character out. (This goes for Shakespeare and contemporary playwrights as well.) By taking this approach, you are guaranteeing that your monologue involves another person from whom you want something and upon whom you are acting.

If you do a great deal of nonmusical acting, you may also want to have a monologue from early Greek or Roman theatre, but normally Shakespeare is enough to suffice for classical or verse pieces. Just do your best to have both a comedic and a dramatic option.

The next thing you'll need is some great realism from the masters of realistic drama. These authors include Henrik Ibsen (*A Doll House, Ghosts, Hedda Gabler*); Anton Chekhov (*The Three Sisters, The Cherry Orchard, Ivanov* [pronounced Ē-van-ov]); Arthur Miller (*Death of a Salesman, All My Sons, The Crucible*); Eugene O'Neill (*Long Day's Journey into Night, A Moon for the Misbegotten, Ah! Wilderness*); Clifford Odets (*Waiting for Lefty, Golden Boy, Awake and Sing!*); Tennessee Williams (*The Glass Menagerie, Cat on a Hot Tin Roof, Suddenly Last Summer, Summer and Smoke*); and for African Americans August Wilson (*Fences, Joe Turner's Come and Gone, The Piano Lesson,* and *Ma Rainey's Black Bottom*).

Chances are, you won't find much in the way of comedic monologues from these writers, but they are important enough figures of dramatic literature that their work will serve you well in auditions. Regardless of whether you find monologues that you like in any number of the titles I have listed above, you should read all of them and be familiar with their plots and characters if you wish to be able to hold a serious discussion about theatre with anyone. In addition to seeking out monologues, you should always be reading plays for your ongoing education. However, I promise you if it is monologues you seek, you will find ample choices in those plays.

Finally, find a piece or two from more contemporary dramatists such as Neil LaBute (*The Shape of Things, Some Girls, Fat Pig*); Kenneth Lonergan (*Lobby Hero, This Is Our Youth*); John Guare (*Six Degrees of Separation, The Loveliest Afternoon of the Year*); Paula Vogel (*The Baltimore Waltz*); David Lindsay-Abaire (*Rabbit Hole, Wonder of the World*); Neil Simon (*Biloxi Blues, Lost in Yonkers*); Richard Greenberg (*Take Me Out*); Brian Friel (*Translations*); and Alfred Uhry (*The Last Night of Ballyhoo*), to name just a few.

You want to find characters who really speak to you, roles you can sink your teeth into right now at this point in your life. And these monologues you seek should never exceed one minute in length. Even when an audition calls for a two-minute monologue, trust me: a minute is as long as they will need to determine if they like you or not. You don't want to wear out your welcome or talk yourself *out* of a callback.

As with music, there are monologues and playwrights you may wish to avoid because they are overdone or badly written. Again, this is only my personal hit list, but you may find that many directors agree with most or all of my selections: Eugene's monologues from *Brighton Beach Memoirs* by Neil Simon, anything from *The Star Spangled Girl* by Neil Simon, the "Jack and Jill" monologues from *Butterflies Are Free* by Leonard Gershe, anything by Christopher Durang or David Ives, *The Diary of Anne Frank*, and Tom's final speech and Laura's "Blue Roses" speech from *The Glass Menagerie* by Tennessee Williams.

The key is to continue reading plays at every chance you get. Read old plays. Read new plays. If you get to New York, visit the Drama Book Shop and check out their "hot new titles" shelves. Scan the cast of characters for roles within your age range and gender and read those plays.

Finally, for every monologue you add to your arsenal, I urge you to type out the speech and keep it in the back of your repertoire book. You never know when you'll be sitting in the waiting room at an audition that only called for a song, and three people ahead of you will walk out lamenting that the director is asking to hear comedic monologues in addition. What a relief that you can pull out any of the pieces you have learned and quickly refresh them before going in to the audition room.

Now you have all the keys to developing and maintaining a well-polished repertoire book. These tips will serve you throughout your entire career, whether you are in high school, college, or the big city. Spend the time thoroughly preparing every piece that you add to your "A" book, and I guarantee you will audition with more polish and confidence than ever before. And directors will notice.

Suit the Word to the Action

Assuming you've developed a thorough repertoire book filled with songs you love to sing (which you sing well), choosing a particular song for a specific audition should be fairly simple. Just remember this bit of advice: *Let the song suit the audition as well as the performer.*

For example, if you are auditioning for a production of *Good News*, a 1920s high school flapper dance musical, you would be best served finding an audition piece that both embodies the spirit and essence of that show and also displays your appropriateness for casting in it. Material from shows such as *The Boy Friend* or *Thoroughly Modern Millie* would be a smart choice, since they are set in the same era with the same style and they contain characters of similar age and type. Material from *Grease*, although it's a high school–age musical, would be wrong because of its 1950s music; and material from *Show Boat*, although it's from the 1920s, is not right because of the completely different ages and types of characters in that show (not to mention the musical's vast stylistic differences).

You show a great deal of professionalism and savvy if you come in to an audition understanding the casting needs of the specific show and choosing material that shows the director how good *you* would be in that production.

3

WALKING THROUGH THE AUDITION

ANYTHING THAT CAN GO WRONG . . .

The nervous actor paces back and forth outside the studio. He is trying—and consistently failing—to review his song lyrics as the tenor in the room begins what the actor is certain is his *third* song. The young man struggles to hear himself think over the beating of his own heartbeat, which is now filling his ears.

The audition called for only 32 bars. What the hell are they doing with him in there? Are they asking everyone to sing more? What else should I sing if they do want another song? I really wasn't intending on having to pick another song. What if they don't ask me to sing more? Does that mean they're not interested in me? I have to nail this audition. I'll just go in there and show them I—

The door opens and the actor is brought back to reality at the sound of his name being called by the monitor. He takes a deep breath and tries to shake his nerves out through his fingertips. He steps into the room and immediately spots the accompanist reading the *Times* drearily at the piano. He makes a beeline to the upright and gently thrusts his music book under the nose of the musician, opening the binder to the last page of "She Loves Me." (He was going to sing "I Met a Girl," but he heard no fewer than three people sing that selection in the hour he'd been waiting!)

"Just start there and go to the end," he tells the pianist, pointing to the red marking on the page. The actor then crosses to the center of the room and for the first time notices the three people sitting behind the table, looking utterly indifferent.

"Should I just start?" He asks, trying to smile confidently.

"Whenever you're ready," replies the man seated at the center of the table. The actor wonders for a moment if this is the director. Should he say something to him? Look at him? Break the ice?

"And tomorrow . . . tomorrow . . . aaaahhhhhhh . . ."

That accompanist just started playing! I wasn't ready. Does he know how ludicrous this must sound, so rushed?

The breathless actor struggles to keep up with the break-neck tempo that this cruel musician has set.

"She . . . loves . . . meeeeeeeeee."

With heart pounding wildly, the young man forces a smile. Had he sung the right words? Was he in tune? It's all a blur to him at this point. No matter, though; it's over. A minor wave of relief washes over the actor. His reverie is broken by the man whom he suspected was the director: "Thank you," the voice intones with a hint of mock-enthusiasm.

"Thank *you*," the actor forces as he turns on his heels to leave, eager to put a great deal of distance between himself and this entire experience. But just as he reaches the door another voice calls out his name. He stops, and in an instant he feels overwhelming redemption.

They did like me. They want me to sing more. They want me to come back here tomorrow and read for the leading role.

"You forgot your music." It's the voice of that damned accompanist who had just ruined the actor's audition. But what can the young man do at this point? Blushing, he smiles awkwardly and retrieves his binder. He is grateful to hear the door close behind him following what has been a painfully long, excruciatingly silent trek to the piano and back out of the room.

He is glad it's over. He packs his book and his water bottle back into his bag and begins the walk back to the midtown office where he is temping for the day. If he walks fast enough, he might still have time before the end of lunch to check the paper for any good auditions the next day.

Depressing, isn't it? And yet, this is a daily occurrence for hundreds of actors in dozens of cities. But it doesn't have to be that way. The actor in the story simply hadn't found the joy in auditioning. He lost sight of his purpose and he dug himself an emotional, psychological abyss before he even stepped into the room. His confidence shot before he began, he didn't stand a chance in there.

A few pieces of advice may have set that poor young man (and multitudes of fellow actors) on a better track to success in the audition room:

Tip 1: Prepare, Prepare, Prepare

I know I'm being redundant, repetitive, and redundant on this point, but it cannot be overemphasized. You *must* know any song in your book by rote. That means you don't have to spend the time leading up to your audition reviewing notes and lyrics. There will never be enough time to cram, and you will forget the song when your nerves kick in. If you know your song backwards and forwards, in your sleep, you can put your focus elsewhere . . . like on the *acting* perhaps!

Further to that point, you'll remember that our tragic hero had originally prepared to sing "I Met a Girl" (a great Golden-Age up-tempo song from *Bells Are Ringing*), but he switched at the last moment to avoid choosing a piece that several others had already gone in with. Switching last-minute would not have been problematic had he been confident with every song in his repertoire. But more poignantly, he shouldn't have been intimidated. If six women sing "I Enjoy Being a Girl," do any of them do it exactly the same? Your job as an actor is to interpret and act every song you perform as though it were happening to you right in that very moment, for the first time. If you can do that, I promise you your rendition will be unique and special. If you can't do that, it doesn't really matter what you sing or how many others sang it before you that day; you'll fall flat. *Just remember, they're auditioning you, not your song.*

Tip 2: Keep Your Focus in the Right Place

Nobody gets cast from a first audition. It just doesn't happen. Your purpose in an audition is to show the auditors you at your very best. Your subliminal message to them is "I am worthy." Getting a callback is the most you can hope to achieve, and it is the measure of a successful audition. If you try to do too much, you'll overshoot the mark and wind up shooting yourself in the foot. Our fictional actor was so concerned with getting the job ("nailing it") and comparing himself with the other actors going in ahead of him that he lost sight of his own mission. Similarly, when actors go in needing a job too much and trying to be exactly what the director wants, it almost guarantees failure. It's as though the directors can smell the neediness, and they immediately reject it.

Besides, you'll never know what they're really after—it's not for you to know, so stop trying to figure it out. Just concentrate on your objective, stay focused, and remain in control. Just relax. Remember that this is your daily opportunity to do what you love—perform. And try not to show them any more than yourself at your very best.

Tip 3: Be a Person in There

An unfortunate majority of actors follow the path of the hypothetical man in my story, from the door to the piano to the 'X' on the floor to the piano to the door, without taking a moment to connect with the auditors on a personal level. Would you put your baby in the care of a rigid automaton that shows no outward display of compassion, empathy, or emotion? Neither would a director.

Stop trying so hard to show them what you *think* they want to see—you will never be able to know what they want or how to manufacture it. Instead, just show them who you are and what you have to offer. Then it's up to them to determine if you match what they are seeking this time around. If you aren't cast, it's no judgment on your talent; but you've done yourself a service by showing them your humanity. I can't tell you how often I pass on an actor because she isn't right for a particular show I'm casting, but I keep her in mind and call her in later for a more suitable role. What makes an actor memorable and impressionable enough to earn casting clout for future projects? *Vulnerability, honesty, and personality.*

Tip 4: Own Your Audition

Nobody in the room wants you to fail. They are trying to cast their show, so your collapse and humiliation benefits nobody, least of all the artistic staff. If you keep that fact in mind and remain in control of your audition from start to finish, you'll greatly improve your chance for success. In the pages that follow, I'll walk you through the steps for controlling your own fate in an audition room, but for now just remember that it's your time.

The performance is only one part of the audition process. Communication makes up a large percentage of the overall experience. As we move forward in the following pages, we'll spend some time dealing with this issue as it pertains to all of the people in the audition room. For now, suffice it to say that if you feel like the pianist is rushing your song and making a mess of your audition, it probably began with poor communication on your part. If you feel as though the auditors are ignoring you and focusing on their fingernails or their lunches, it probably began with poor communication on your part.

A VERY GOOD PLACE TO START

There's an old saying in the theatre that goes, Your audition begins the moment you walk in the door. This point cannot be overstated. Many actors feel that they need to deal with the accompanist first and get their bearings before being ready to face the panel. This is a major fallacy. The director has a very limited amount of time to gather as much information as possible about you. Although this information includes singing and acting ability, it also comprises a great deal of personal information. The director wants to know if you have a sense of humor, if you are outgoing, if you are confident, if you are intelligent, if you can be present and compelling. If you walk into the room silently, with your head down, and march directly to the accompanist, the director learns little about you beyond a certain ability to radiate anxiety.

Why not use every second to your advantage? Impress them before they even hear you sing. Have them liking you so much that they think "God, I hope she can sing!" This process begins by *owning the room*. It is your audition, and you must appear as though you are in control of the entire process. Nothing surprises you or throws you. When you walk through the door, walk in as though you were meant to be there. Carry an air of confidence and warmth that emanates through the room and makes them relax. Always begin by acknowledging everyone in the room with a polite, "Hello, how are you?" This is, at the very least, a basic courtesy you would extend to a room of people in any given situation, especially one in which you are seeking a job offer. After all, directors, pianists, and choreographers are people too, and we don't want to feel we've been treated rudely.

From this point on, you must engage and remain in active listening mode. You may run into a sullen room of people who are holding conference and ignoring you when you enter: Just move on. You may find that they perk up upon hearing your polite greeting and respond with further conversation. Use it. You may simply get a curt grunt with no encouragement to take the chatting any further: Don't let it throw your routine. Whatever the case, you should remain open and respond to whatever they throw at you. If they want to talk to you, don't run to the piano and anxiously try to move things along. Stop and talk to them—you may be the only one all day who has! The more they can get to know you outside of your performance, the better. The bottom line is: *always remain present in the audition room*. It's part of the test of a good actor, this ability to be present. Additionally, the mantra of the audition should be "face time." The more they get of you and your face as a first impression, the better. So if they want to talk, let them talk to you.

That said, be careful not to overdo it. Some actors try to be too chummy with me in an audition, and it's a big turnoff. Don't start telling jokes and being cute; don't *ever*, under any circumstances, go for an unsolicited hand-shake—in fact, it's best if you do not ever approach the table unless you are asked to do so; don't ask personal questions, including the ever-popular "Are you having a great day so far?"; and in general, don't try to drag out more dialog than they're willing to exchange with you. Again, just let them take the lead on whether or not there will be conversation, and be open and responsive to what they give you. They may ask how you're doing. They may ask you personal questions. If so, they just want to get to know you. So don't try to put on an act for them. Save that for your audition pieces.

When David Rotenberg teaches his course on film acting in Toronto, he tells his students that their job on camera is to "always be present." He likens the actor to an athlete, stating that "a ball player couldn't hit a base-ball traveling at 95 miles per hour if he weren't present." This is exactly the kind of focus you must have in an audition for the theatre. If you're up in your head looking for song lyrics, or you're thinking about what you're going to do once it's over, or you're wondering what the choreographer is thinking as she gapes wide-mouthed at you while you sing your high notes, then you are not present. You cannot act well and stay in the moment if you're not present, and you certainly won't do well at light, personal banter before or after your audition pieces. If, however, you can make those audi-tors feel as though they are the most important people in the world to you right now and their project is worthy of all of your attention right now, then you are sufficiently present. Concurrently, if you can deal with them on a personal level and really be yourself up until the moment when you begin your first audition piece—resuming that sense of self after you finish your piece—then you are sufficiently present as well. It's no easy task, but if this were easy, everyone would do it! It will take a great deal of practice and some degree of failure before you nail down these concepts and put them into practice efficiently.

One more thought on *when* your audition actually begins: Sometimes your audition may begin *before* you walk in the door. If you are in the wait-ing room and one or more of the artistic staff comes into the room on a break, in a small sense, you are auditioning for them. If you pass the direc-tor in the hallway and smile at him, in a small sense, you are auditioning for him. If you are at a college entrance audition and the head of the program addresses the entire group of potential students before the dance combination is taught, in a sense, you are auditioning for her. The point is, don't let your guard down. Be on your best behavior and always be aware of who is around you. You don't want to begin your audition carrying the stigma of "the guy who was chatting while the director was giving instructions to everyone." Be attentive, and by all means *be nice to everyone!* I'm certainly not suggesting you become sycophantic or disingenuous, and I do not want to discourage you from being bold and daring in an audition; rather, I want you to avoid being rude or offensive outside of the audition room. You really never know with whom you may be speaking.

PLAY ME THE MUSIC

I am not exaggerating when I tell you that the piano player should be your best friend in the audition room. I say "should" because whether he is or not is entirely up to you. But if you play your cards right, you may gain a major ally in your audition. Whether a piano player is attached to a project, or (as is more often the case in professional auditions) he is hired just for the day to accompany auditions, he is an extremely important figure. Think about it: if you are auditioning for a musical, this person is literally your partner through the singing portion. Yet countless people, just like the unfortunate guy in our story, treat the accompanist as some sort of servant whose job it is to play what you set in front of them, no questions asked.

I'll let you in on a little secret, though: piano players are human beings, too. Although you may not require their approval to be cast in a production, treating them disrespectfully can be a major detriment to your job hopes. Besides the fact that many of them will tell the director what a jerk you are if you mistreat them, there's also the risk that they won't put very much effort into helping you succeed in your performance. Talking down to them, snapping your fingers at them, and generally treating them like they aren't there is the best way to ensure you'll get no extra help from them.

On the other hand, think of how much a good accompanist can help your cause if he decides to really follow you as you audition. If he is sympathetic to your nerves and in tune with your rhythms, it becomes like a scene with the two of you playing off of each other. The best thing an accompanist can tell you after you finish your audition is that he had fun playing for you. Chances are, if he says this, then you had fun as well and so did the director. So why not go for this optimal experience every time? It isn't hard to ensure a happy pianist—it just takes a touch of personalization and humanity, not to mention a wonderfully organized repertoire binder with music in nonglare sheets.

Once you have entered the room and acknowledged everyone behind the table with a cordial greeting, you'll be given time to confer with the accompanist before you introduce your pieces and sing. When you get to the piano, be sure to talk to the accompanist in a position that allows the artistic staff to see your face, not your back side (remember: face time). Make sure you greet the piano player genuinely and kindly—he's been working harder than anyone else in the room all day, and he'll appreciate your sincerity. This is where owning your audition comes into play. Make certain that you communicate exactly what you need from the pianist in the audition. Begin by gently displaying your music in front of him and telling him what song(s) you'll be singing. More often than not, the accompanist will be familiar with your selections, but either way, it's always good to start by saying "I'm going to sing 'Such and Such' from the musical *So and So.*" This way you can make certain the pianist knows what he's being asked to play, especially if you're starting from a point other than the first page.

The next pieces of information you'll need to convey are your starting and ending points as well as any jumps or repeats you'll need him to take. Unless you're going straight through from beginning to end with no repeats or cuts whatsoever, all of this information should be clearly marked with your marker and highlighter for ease of sight-reading, and you should take the time to point it out to the pianist. Further, don't assume that because you've marked a cut in your music the musician will be able to follow you on the spot without some warning. Cover your bases and talk it through, making sure that you are clear about how you want to sing the song.

Tell him how you want to begin. Frequently, an actor will wish to begin in the middle of a song or skip any musical introduction at the top. It is common in these cases to ask the pianist to start you off with a chord or a starting pitch, so that you know what note to come in on. If you do not ask for one, you should assume that the accompanist will play exactly whatever intro music is written, and you may find yourself standing there waiting for the song to come around to your entrance. Be sure you know what you want going in, and practice it that way.

Next, you need to convey the tempo. Don't assume the accompanist knows how you do your song, even if—as is often the case—he tells you "I know it" when you put it in front of him. Everyone takes songs at their own tempos, so you must make certain that you and the pianist are in-sync about this information. Most pianists I've ever known prefer that you don't snap at them and count (*one two three, one two three*) to establish your tempo.

Rather, they appreciate when you sing a little snippet of the song to them while tapping the piano top or your leg, so that they can hear exactly how you intend to sing the piece. Just a couple of lines will usually do, unless of course, there is a change of tempo somewhere in the song; in which case, you'll want to point this out as well. There may also be times when you'll want the pianist to follow you—for instance if a song begins freely before the rhythm is established. Again, make sure you are clear with him that this is your expectation, and be specific about when you want the song to be played at tempo. Beware of nerves during this conversation. Many actors, jittery and anxious, end up setting a brutally fast tempo (probably matching their heartbeat) and then struggle to keep up. *It's usually a good idea to suggest a slightly slower tempo than you actually think you want.* With practice, you'll find out how best to handle this exchange.

If there is a modulation (key change) or any other oddities in the song, you also want to bring that to the pianist's attention and have it highlighted in the sheet music as well, so that they are warned in advance and can continue to follow you.

So thus far, you have a good deal of information to present at the piano. The good news is, most of it is printed or marked on the page; you only need to point the pianist's attention to it and you're covered. In a worst-case scenario, you forget to mention a key or time change, and the accompanist stutters and then makes the adjustment. Give most piano players the benefit of the doubt that they are there because they can competently read music. However, there is one piece of information that cannot be found anywhere in the sheet music, which you *must* remember to address before you begin. Remember what happened to the actor when the song just started playing with no warning? This common snafu can be avoided by establishing a starting signal with the accompanist.

Some people prefer to nod in the direction of the piano, indicating readiness. This method brings the actor out of focus from the start and it usually takes a good five seconds before she finds the character in the song (especially when the piano is behind her in the audition room, causing her to start with her focus upstage). Others will actually count in the song—I don't need to tell you why this is a bad idea. A better alternative would be to ask the pianist to wait just a second after you are done introducing your piece(s) and then begin. This way, you are in character from the get-go, and the pianist will clearly know that you are ready to perform. You'd be surprised at how effectively an inhalation can signal the upbeat preceding the downbeat of your music if you and the accompanist are really connected. Whatever way you choose to begin, just make sure to let the pianist know so he doesn't have to guess—for example, "Start when I stomp my foot on the ground and yell 'wowzer!'" or "I'll inhale for an upbeat after I introduce myself."

If you can communicate your needs politely and thoroughly to the accompanist, you give yourself a major advantage before you even sing a note. If your music is cleanly photocopied, marked appropriately, placed in nonglare sheets in a binder, and set up for the fewest page turns, you will appear extremely polished and professional. If you calmly walk the piano player through exactly what he'll need to know to play your music well, you will make a great impression and he will try hard for you. He may even put in a good word with the director.

Finally, if you are singing multiple songs or doing a monologue as well, do all of your instructing to the pianist before you begin the actual audition. Just tell him in what order you plan to perform your pieces and how you will signal him to begin each of your songs. Once you introduce yourself and begin to perform, you won't want to lose your momentum and have to return to the piano. Believe me when I tell you that all of this thorough attention to detail on your part can enhance your chances of success tenfold.

So let me summarize what may have seemed like a very long process. You greet the pianist. You tell him what songs you are singing. You show him starting and ending points along with any cuts, jumps, or repeats. You explain a tempo. You ask for a starting note, a chord, or the written introduction. And you tell him when you want him to start playing. I also think it's a good idea to ask if the piano player has any questions when you are finished explaining everything. Finally, and most importantly, thank the pianist before you walk away to sing. A little courtesy goes a long way in this business.

This entire exchange needs to be both thorough and quick. You do not want to keep the auditors waiting long. I suggest you always spend time practicing this exchange at the piano so that you have it streamlined down to an art. Let's take a look at an example:

> Good afternoon. How are you? I'll be singing "Brother, Can You Spare a Dime." Do you know it? I'm starting here at the bridge and going straight through to the end here. There's a modulation into the last verse. And I take it at this tempo [I sing a bit and tap my leg]. And if you could please play me the first chord after I finish introducing myself to them, I'll take a breath and come in. Do you have any questions? All right. Thank you so much.

Read that paragraph out loud. How long did it take to get through all of that information? 20 seconds? 25? Even if you have something a little more complicated or if you have a second song to explain, it is imperative that the exchange at the piano not be much longer than that. Again, practicing this little speech and marking everything clearly will make for the smoothest interaction.

COMMUNICATIONS BREAKDOWN

No matter how thorough you are about your instruction to the pianist—no matter how good the pianist may sight-read—there is always the chance that things will go wrong. In a perfect world, assuming you follow all of my prepping guidelines, you should sail through the audition. But let's face it, it's not a perfect world and not every accompanist you meet will be Sondheim. Many of them won't even be able to play Sondheim!

Keep one phrase firmly planted in your humble mind for those days when you encounter the musician who is all knuckles at the ivories:

"Sorry, my fault."

I know what you're thinking: "But it isn't my fault. This guy is playing a cut-time like it's a slow waltz! He can't read!"

"Sorry, my fault."

"I told her to give me a chord after I say, 'Yee haw,' and she just started playing the damn song before I could even draw a breath!"

"Sorry, my fault."

You take responsibility for your entire audition and they'll know you're a pro. Any director will understand a shaky start. If you need to stop and start over in order to straighten things out with the pianist, they'll allow it one time, penalty-free, if you take the responsibility. See friends, here's the trick: If the pianist is lousy or simply gets a bad start on your piece, chances are, everyone in the room knows it. You only show yourself as rude and unsympathetic by leveling blame or dirty looks in the general direction of the piano. If, however, you excuse yourself and restore communication in a nonconfrontational way, I promise you they will respect you for it and forgive the false start. Not to mention that the pianist will likely redouble his effort on your behalf.

And if it is simply not your day and you'd be better served with a monkey at the piano, it is necessary for you to bite the bullet and plow through your audition after one start-over, or just present the song a cappella. For, in the end, the pianist is not being auditioned; you are. So just sing your song, trying your utmost to work with what the musician is offering, and make sure to *stay in character* and remain gracious. Most likely the director will

know that the pianist is at fault for the bad accompaniment, and your audition won't be a wash. The surefire way to run your audition into the ground
is to snap, throw dirty looks, roll your eyes, or make comments about the
pianist. So don't do it.

I don't mean to frighten you by making the accompanist sound like
a terrifying menace who's likely to bring you down. Moreover, I hope
that any pianist reading this chapter understands that my experience has
found these monstrous musicians to be a small minority. Most pianists
are absolutely capable and eager to help you succeed even if you toss a
softbound, unmarked anthology of songs in front of them without so much
as a word of explanation. I've never seen a piano player throw her hands
up in disgust and bang the keys in rage when a foolish actor has brought
loose, unattached sheet music to an audition and it starts to find its way
all over the floor of the studio. Musicians are certainly not unsympathetic
to the artist's plight, and they will do their best to help you as much as
they can. It's just important that you be sensitive to their needs and that
you go in prepared to face minor setbacks. They're infrequent, but they
do happen. You greatly lower the odds of meltdown by being organized
and professional.

AND NOW INTRODUCING . . .

You're off to a great start. You've walked in, smiled and greeted the auditors, and headed to the piano. You've given the pianist your music and
talked him through tempos, starting points, key changes, and so on. Now
you find yourself standing before the table, ready to plunge headlong into
your audition performance and blow them away. It only remains for you to
introduce yourself and your pieces.

Believe it or not, this simple statement of who you are and what you're
going to present seems to cause a great deal of grief for many actors. What
exactly *are* you supposed to say before you begin? Should you tell them
what musical your selection is from? Should you tell them which character
you'll be portraying, or perhaps offer a little bit of set-up information? I've
seen auditions in which the actor took more time explaining her monologue
than actually reciting it. Should you introduce all of your pieces at the beginning or is it better to present the titles individually before you perform
each of them?

I'm going to give you an easy default method to practice—and you *should*
practice it, as it is part of the audition, and nerves can screw you up even

on something as basic as an introduction. Then we'll discuss some possible variables.

For starters, always make certain you have their attention before you begin. Often, they'll be discussing or taking notes about the person who came before you when you step in front of them. Stand there patiently, be sure to smile, and wait until they have given you their eye contact or informed you that they are ready for you. This way, you avoid them missing any part of your audition and you don't make them feel rushed.

If you've already exchanged a "hello" or "good morning" on your entrance, do not repeat it when you begin to audition. If you did not exchange any pleasantries when you walked in the room, once you have their attention, begin by greeting them appropriately (good morning/afternoon/evening) and then wait for just a second for them to respond to you. Usually they'll simply return your greeting and then you should continue your introduction. But occasionally they may ask how you are doing or make other conversation. Be open to this possibility and don't be thrown if they take you in an unexpected direction—just go with it. (Remember: be present.)

Assuming they don't offer anything more than a grunt when you greet them, move on to your name. You must learn to state your name slowly, clearly, and with confidence. It's amazing how we take something so common for granted, but you'd be surprised at how many people slur and butcher their own names, rendering them unintelligible. Sometimes, I've even had to look at the résumé in front of me to understand the name that has just been stated, which of course causes me to miss the next portion of their introduction. Many actors drop out in vocal energy at the ends of lines, so we hear "Hi, I'm Jesse John—" (instead of Jesse Johnson). The other common faux pas with the name is to give it the inflection of a question. You know the type: "Hi, I'm Jesse Johnson?" I know I'm being nitpicky, but it really makes a difference if you can state your name positively and let it land.

Finally, introduce your pieces. The best advice I can offer here is the old K.I.S.S. method (Keep it simple, stupid.). Just tell them what they need to know, nothing more. If you're singing one song, all you need to say is "this is 'Such and Such.'" If you're singing two songs, similarly, you just tell them "this is 'Such and Such' and 'What's it Called.'" Note: always introduce all your pieces at the top. It goes back to that point I made earlier of not wanting to lose your momentum once you begin. If you are doing a monologue as well, you can say something like "I'll be doing a monologue from *The Great Play* and singing 'Song of the World.'" Or you can simply say "This is *The Great Play*, 'Song of the World,' and 'She Wishes She Were Me.'"

But that's really all they need to know from you. In most cases, they either know what show the song is from already or they don't care. If they want to know what it's from or which character sings it, or who wrote it, they'll ask you: just another golden opportunity to engage in conversation with them. Otherwise, just keep it simple. The more information you try to cram, the further you get from having their premium attention spans. Let's look at an example. It may help you to read this out loud, making sure to observe the punctuation carefully, so you get a sense of how a good introduction might sound: "Good afternoon. (pause) I'm Jonathan Flom. And this is 'Tonight at Eight' and 'Brother, Can You Spare a Dime.'"

What could be easier? Notice that I use a period following "good afternoon" as well as after I state my name. This allows them to respond to my greeting and it also lets my name land in their ears before I offer my song selections. Notice also that I remove the question mark that naturally follows the title of my second song. Again, I want to sound confident and sure. I don't want them to respond with "Are you?" after I say I'm singing "Brother, Can You Spare a *Dime*?" Finally, my deliberate pacing and pausing allows them to write down my choices before I speed on into the singing.

It really should be that simple. A concise introduction allows you to quickly and smoothly get to the heart of your audition. It will grab their attention, and it will make you look polished and professional, as long as you have rehearsed it enough before going in.

As I said, that's the default intro. Let's discuss some variables that require slight adjustments:

Before I begin my introduction, the director says, "Hello Jonathan. How are you today?"

Remember to be present and deal with the auditors as though they are human beings. If they greet you, listen and respond appropriately. Most likely they'll have your name on a list and your résumé in front of them. If they do refer to you by your name, it is redundant to then go ahead and introduce yourself. It's certainly not necessary to tell them your name once they address you and establish that they know who you are. This is particularly the case when the auditors know you—they are your teachers or you've worked with them before. No introduction is necessary with these folks. As a director, I tend to break the ice in an effort to keep things more casual and help the actor feel comfortable. I'll usually address the actor by name, ask how she is, and ask what she's going to sing for us before she goes through the motions of a rigid introduction. If she still gives me her standard intro, I know she is not truly present. This gives me a chance to share some dialogue with the actor and to see if she listens and responds to me. Be open to conversation.

I started to introduce myself and they asked me to back up a few steps.

The people behind the table want to see all of you. They are essentially sizing you up and trying to imagine how you will look on stage in their production. Getting too close to the table inhibits their ability to really look at you. It also tends to make directors feel crowded and uncomfortable. Often there will be a line or an 'X' taped on the floor. You should always look down to see if they have marked a spot and then stay behind it. If there is no mark, try to remain 10 to 12 feet from the auditors' table. And if you are like me and have lousy depth perception, just be sure they can see your feet without having to lean forward across the table. If you move around during your audition, try to always leave at least this much distance between you and the table and don't encroach upon the staff. The farther the better, I always say.

When I introduced my audition selections, they asked if I had something else instead.

This is a rare occurrence, but I have seen it happen. Once in a while, a director will be straightforward enough to tell you in advance that the song you have selected will not sufficiently show her what she wants to see from you—a sort of directorial cut-to-the-chase, if you will. Although it doesn't happen often (more commonly, you'll finish your song and then they'll ask you for something different), it is important to arrive armed and ready for such an artistic assault from the director. Here's how you handle it:

When you go to an audition, choose the song or songs you plan to sing, but also choose at least two possible options in case they ask for something else. When they say, "Do you have another song?" you can then offer them options: "Absolutely. I have 'Bill' (*Show Boat*) and I have 'I Wanna Be Bad.' (*Good News*) What would you like to hear?"

Then it's back in their hands. They either choose a song you offer (Oh, how prepared you look!), or they ask, "What else?" If they ask that question, you have permission to go back to the piano and flip through your book until you hit on something they like. Sometimes they're looking for something very specific, and having several options will increase your chances of showing it to them.

Just remember that if they ask for a different song, you'll need to return to the accompanist and walk him through the new selection for tempos, starting point, and so on.

I followed your advice and said "I am . . . and this is . . . ," and they imme-diately asked me to tell them what show it was from and who wrote it.

This is not a bad thing. You did not make a mistake by omitting that information. Sometimes they don't really need to know what show or what composers; they're just testing you to see if you know, or they are making conversation to get you to speak more. Either way, don't panic. As long as you have done all your homework when preparing your repertoire book, questions like this shouldn't throw you. Just be sure you don't stammer when asked, or worse, mispronounce names of composers or lyricists (re-member: Jule Styne is pronounced "Julie").

There aren't too many other variables that I can think of to offer you. Most of the time, you'll be able to get up there, greet them, introduce yourself and your pieces, and fly. But as long as you are always open to deal *enthusiastically* with whatever is thrown at you, you will be fine.

THE TWO-MINUTE DRILL

We're now ready to deal with the meat of the audition: the performance. Interestingly, by the time you arrive at this point, there is very little that you can do to control your fate. You either sing the notes well or you don't; you either make compelling acting choices or you don't; they either think you're right for the role or they don't. With the exception of role appropriateness, which is completely out of your hands, everything rests on the preparation you have done leading up to this moment. If you have trained your body, voice, and imagination; if you've read and understood the audition call; if you've invested in good headshots and created a clean, polished résumé; if you've prepared your repertoire book professionally and chosen selections that show you off at your best; if you've entered the room confidently and dealt with everyone in a proper manner, then what remains to be done should be a cakewalk. Stand and deliver, as the saying goes. And have fun up there.

There are a few guidelines I can offer to help you get the most mileage out of your audition performance, but even most of these suggestions go back to preparation. The bottom line is, you want to do all of your work before the audition, then stay out of your own way once you're in there. The minute you get up in your head (i.e., wondering if they like you, thinking about correct lyrics, judging your performance), you cease to be present and you run into trouble. That said, here are some bits of audition wisdom to consider:

I. The First 30 Seconds Is Everything

It's cliché, I know, but some people are even less generous and make their decision after about 15 seconds. Directors who have done their homework know pretty well what they want, and although they won't be so rash as to cast someone based on 20 seconds of a song, they can generally decide in that time frame if they *don't* want someone. Many students ask me what they should lead with: Up-tempo or ballad? Comedic or dramatic? Monologue or song? The answer depends on what you're auditioning for and which material you're auditioning with. And the best advice I can offer is get 'em hooked quickly. The notion of "save the best for last" has no place at an audition. Ed Linderman suggests you try to use an uplifting, joyous, or fun song as a first impression, and then wow them with your dramatic, balladic acting chops for the second song or at the callback. I can't say I disagree with this philosophy.

As an example, if you are auditioning for a belting role, and you've chosen to sing "Gimme, Gimme" from *Thoroughly Modern Millie* and "Bewitched" from *Pal Joey* as your contrasting piece, it makes the most sense to lead with "Gimme, Gimme" and show them your belt skills right away. You should also be sure you cut the song so that you get to the belted notes quickly.

If they want to hear more, they'll ask you to go back, but chances are, they're just interested to hear if you can sing those powerful notes. Why make them wait? You may encounter a casting director who is pressed for time, only to find that they cut you off before you get to your "money notes" and you never get to show them what you came to do.

Another side of the order-of-pieces issue arises when you are auditioning for "style" pieces. Often a call for a Shakespearean production will require a song, since many of his plays include music. In these cases, the emphasis is obviously on handling verse language, so the monologue should take priority. Use your common sense when you approach an audition and you will do fine. Know what you are going in for and lead with the primary casting point for that particular project.

2. Unless You Are Singing Pop, Rock, or Country Music, Always, Always Act the Song

A pretty voice is one thing, but good musical theatre demands more. Acting is what separates good musical productions from bad ones. You must make solid acting choices for every theatrical song you sing and fully invest in the character. Ask yourself these questions for every musical theatre song in your repertoire:

Who am I?

To whom am I singing?

What do I want from this person? (If I could write the end of the scene, my scene partner would _____.)

What is my obstacle?

What tactics can I use to overcome the obstacle? Tactics are the actions an actor uses to achieve his goal (to tease, to flirt, to seduce, to lecture, to soothe, etc.). They should always be active verbs.

These are the most basic building blocks to scene work, and they must be applied to musical theatre to make it rise above meaningless fluff. I strongly urge you to read *A Practical Handbook for the Actor* (Bruder et al.) as well as *Sanford Meisner on Acting*. These two books offer the most complete system for truthful acting, and their methods can and should be utilized in musicals as well. In the meantime, the following is an example for you to consider.

Every actor should have one tried-and-true, standby audition piece—a song that you know and love better than any other, and one that you can pull out for virtually any audition and feel confident: your "ace." My ace song is "Brother, Can You Spare a Dime?" from *Americana*. The piece is from the 1930s and the character is a man who helped build this great country and now finds himself out of work and penniless in the Depression. Whenever I sing the song, I am very clear about my acting choices.

I am Al, a hard-working, blue-collar American. I have spent my youth building railroads and skyscrapers in order to make my country great. Now I am unemployed and waiting in line just to receive a ration of bread. The people whom I am singing to are the well-dressed, upper-class passers-by as I wait in the street for my turn in the bread line. I want one of them, just one of them, to hear my story and to offer me some money in appreciation for all the work I did for my country. My obstacle is that people don't see the man I used to be; they only see the homeless bum in dirty tatters asking for a handout. And so the tactics I utilize to overcome my obstacle include

6. Don't Be Afraid to Just Plant Yourself

Standing solidly on two feet and not fidgeting is a sign of confidence and strength. You certainly don't need to remain rooted in place throughout your entire audition; however, you want to find moments when you are able to display stillness—in particular, when you introduce yourself at the top.

Once you are engaged in your songs and monologues, be sure that any movement you make is character driven. In other words, don't pace aimlessly back and forth. If you choose to pace the floor, it must be as a result of a chosen action, for example, *My character is diligently trying to sort out a complicated dilemma.*

Similarly, if you perform a song that specifically requires dance in the lyrics or it's naturally implied in the accompaniment ("What Do I Need with Love" from *Millie*; "All I Need Is the Girl" from *Gypsy*; "I Can't Stand Still" from *Footloose*; "Hit Me with a Hot Note" by Duke Ellington), you should feel free to move a bit, especially if you want to show the director that you are a dancer. But again, it must be character driven and it must fit the circumstances rather than simply being a nervous twitch. Furthermore, you must be able to perform the song without the movement if asked to do so.

When I was recruiting for Penn State's BFA program, we had a handsome, talented young man come in and sing a peppy Gershwin tune—I think it may have been "I've Got Rhythm." He was snapping his fingers and bopping his head and shuffling his feet as though he were auditioning for America's Next Top Crooner! We liked him, but we asked him to take the song again and lose the dancing. He started over, only to pick right back up with the swinging routine.

"Just stand still," we told him. "Understand?"

"Yep," he said nervously.

Once again, the piano player launched into the song. The boy began this time with just a subtle pulsing in his knee to keep time, but it soon led to toe tapping, and before long he was right back at square one.

It was somewhat laughable at the time, as you can imagine. But it was indicative of more than a simple case of nerves on that poor young man's part. He had practiced his song as an entertaining bit of musical frivolity, learning to hide his jitters behind some simple dance moves. But he invested absolutely nothing in the lyrics, meaning, and acting of the song. Again, *any movement must be character motivated.*

7. Say "Yes" to Direction

The undoing of the bouncing boy was not his poor and utter lack of acting choices. It was his unwillingness or inability to take direction when it was offered. His audition was a "frozen" act, unchangeable despite the response from his audience (or scene partner). This is not acting, it's dead! Because he could not make adjustments to his routine, despite multiple attempts on the auditors' part to help him, he became uncastable.

It is not uncommon for a director to ask an actor to make a different choice, in order to see if the actor can take direction. If you find yourself in such a situation, no matter how bizarre you find the director's adjustment to be (e.g., "Can you do the piece again and wring this piece of cloth in your hands as you sing it?"), the appropriate response is, "Yes, I can do that." Of course, the second part of the equation requires that you actually make the adjustment, but having a positive attitude is definitely half the battle.

Inexperience causes many actors to seize up with fear when a director asks them to approach a piece differently than they have rehearsed it. They jump to the conclusion that they've done it wrong or badly. These actors fail to embrace the golden opportunity they have been given: first, a chance to show they are directable, and second, more face time with the director. In this respect, an adjustment is almost as good as a callback, and that is the goal of any audition!

8. Do Not Apologize for Your Work

The only apology you are allowed to offer in an audition is the aforementioned accompanist-music-meltdown humility. Beyond that, you must present a confident, positive image. This means *eliminating any and all excuses* from the audition studio.

Do not try to explain how sick you've been when you arrive with a husk in your voice. Do not try to explain how the trains were all delayed when you arrive late. Do not try to explain why you messed up when you forget your lyrics or botch an audition piece. It is so tempting to want to convince the director that she is not seeing you in optimum performance mode at the moment and that you can do better. I assure you this is self-destructive, so don't do it.

If you are sick or recovering from illness, you have two options: Either skip the auditioning and wait until you are well enough to resume performing again or go in there and sell them on the idea that this is how you sound and you're proud of it. Directors are not stupid. If you are sick, chances are they'll recognize it. They may ask you if you are under the weather (in which case, of course, you answer honestly without embellishing), and they may ask you to reaudition when you have recovered. But whatever they do, they will respect you for putting on a brave face and being a professional. Truth be told, it's often all in your mind that you don't sound healthy. Many actors are surprised to find that they have earned a callback in spite of congestion or other symptoms. It's not usually as detrimental as one might assume. I've seen some of the most interesting acting choices made by the actor who was sick and had to concentrate on something other than the quality of her voice. You should work on learning to sing through illness. Sometimes it requires an extra hour of warm-up; sometimes it means leaning over hot water and steaming. You need to discover what works for you and be sure to fully prepare for any audition you attend.

As for running late, the best thing I can tell you is *don't. You must arrive early to auditions and rehearsals.* Tardiness is not tolerated in this business, and it will lose you jobs if you develop a reputation. In the event that you are unavoidably delayed, try to call the studio and get a message to the monitor—it may be possible to have your slot moved to a later time if you are courteous enough to call and give notice. If you can't call ahead, your options are to show up late and hope for the best or skip the audition all together. If you do decide to go in late, just say, "Sorry I'm late," and leave it at that; no proverbial song and dance. No matter how good (or true) your story is, the minute you begin making an excuse, you dig yourself into a hole.

The other apology I see actors make regularly is the old "I blew that one." This destructive little gem can be blatant—the actor finishes his piece and then verbally comments on his own performance—or it can be subtle and even subconscious—the actor rolls his eyes or laughs, signaling an acknowledgement of his failure. Eliminate these tics from your work. I don't care if you completely forget your words, sing off-key, or trip over your feet in the dance call; you just keep going like you meant for it to be that way. You don't need to tell them you messed up—they'll know it or they may have missed it completely. Either way, you need to demonstrate that you can recover from a mistake. After all, that is what you'd be expected to do during a live performance. If you can do that, I promise you any error you made in your audition will likely fade into nothing.

PUT IT TOGETHER AND . . .

I realize that I have given you a whole lot of information to process, digest, and carry with you through every audition. What's more, I'm telling you that you must stay out of your own head whenever you perform. The only possible way to achieve such synthesis is to practice . . . a lot! You will have off days and failures, but if you take the time to reflect after the fact and make your next audition sharper, then nothing is lost. Think of the baseball player who leads the league with a .333 batting average. He *fails* two-thirds of the time he comes to the plate! But he improves by reflecting on the mechanics involved in his failed at-bats and by making adjustments in the future. The same technique can work for the actor.

As I have said, thorough preparation will really carry you through a smooth audition. If you have walked through everything from dealing with the accompanist, to introducing yourself, to performing your pieces, you won't have to keep focusing on all my little rules and tips in the audition room: It will all become second nature. Once it is, you will be free to have fun in your auditions; believe it or not, this *is* possible!

In preparing my book, I shared some of this chapter's material with a BFA classmate of mine who has been making a steady living on national tours and regional theatre for the last nine years. As we talked through all of these guidelines for handling the audition, he actually told me that he hadn't *thought* about any of it for probably the last seven years or more. It has all become so engrained in him through experience that he is free to relax and really fly through his audition performance. He also told me that as he's gotten to know more and more casting directors in New York, he's felt increasingly confident in taking bigger risks and having more fun when he goes in for them.

It really is simple, this daily grind that performing artists put themselves through. When you follow Meisner's acting advice and put your attention on your actions and your objectives, you will be truly free to perform. Self-consciousness is literally an awareness of one's self. It logically follows that placing your consciousness elsewhere would then alleviate the symptoms associated with self-consciousness. And once you can embrace the audition as your daily chance to do what you love to do, then your joy will be contagious and directors will want to work with you.

THANK YOU FOR LETTING ME . . .

The final step in navigating a successful audition is getting out of the room gracefully. I liken it to an Olympic gymnast who, in order to earn deserved high marks for a killer floor demonstration, must be sure to "stick the landing." Likewise, you must "stick the landing" at the conclusion of your audition and eliminate the awkwardness as you go to exit. But how?

First, think of the wrap-up as just another transition. Only this time, instead of going from one selection to another, you're going from performing a character role back to being your gracious self. The easiest way—really, the only way—to make this segue is to button your final piece, take a beat to let it land, and then say, "Thank you." No further discussion is required on your end; no "that's all" or "scene," or any other extraneous commentary. Just a simple "thank you" and a smile will do.

The mistake that so many novice performers make is that they try to flee the scene as quickly as possible once they complete their audition. I have literally had to chase down actors outside the studio just to ask them some questions following their audition. So stay put for a couple of seconds after you thank them. Nine times out of ten, someone behind the table will return your thanks, and a nod or a smile will indicate that they are finished with you. However, you have to remain open to the possibility that they may want to interview you or even to hear you sing more. (Remember: be present.)

Don't get me wrong, I'm not suggesting that you hang around until they finally have to ask you to leave. It's a delicate balance, but you have to learn just when to head for the door. It's basically a matter of being able to read people. For example, if you finish your last piece and you find them whispering or passing notes or examining your résumé without a word in your direction, you may assume that there is a possibility they'll have something more for you. In such a case, just hang tight until their attention returns to you.

Otherwise, say your "thank you," allow them a beat to respond, and once they have done so, head for the piano to retrieve your music. Do not neglect to thank the pianist as you take your book.

The walk out of the room can feel like a long, awkward silence for everyone. So move with purpose, but don't run. You may want to be careful about wearing shoes that "clump" at an audition; you wouldn't believe how pronounced this noise becomes in a quiet, hardwood-floored room! When you reach the door, you can thank them once more or wish them a good afternoon. It's never a bad idea to leave them with a cordial smile as you exit. But don't say more than that. They are very busy, and you don't want to overstay your welcome.

The bottom line is: Just as the audition begins when you walk in the door, it continues until you walk out the door. So keep your game face on until they've finished seeing the back of you. Furthermore, avoid commenting on your work outside of the studio. I hear many performers, before the door is even closed behind them, sharing the horrors of their auditions with friends in the hallway. I don't want to hear how you "sucked in there" or "what a stone-faced jerk" the director was or "how lousy the accompanist played." Save it for your cell phone on the walk home, once you are clear of the audition building. Until that point, just smile and tell anyone who asks that it went well. It's the professional thing to do, and it avoids the possibility of saying anything damaging within earshot of the wrong person.

Finally, once you're clear of the audition room, *let it go*. You have now done everything you possibly could do as a first step toward booking a job. It is no longer in your hands. You may choose to reflect briefly on whether you thought you performed at your best, but not for more than a moment. You should also take that moment while the information is fresh to add an entry to your journal: who was in the room, what you sang, how it went. But then you must let it go. I know I keep telling you that the goal is a callback, but even that is out of your hands at this point. Instead of harping on what you could have done or should have done in there, go treat yourself to a coffee or an ice cream and a good book, or something else you love. You prepared, went in there, and showed them that you love performing. Now it's up to them to decide if you are what they need. Reward yourself for going in there prepared and doing your best; this way, you will always look forward to auditioning.

SUMMARY

- You can't be too prepared! Know your songs well enough that you don't need to think about them before going in. Relax and focus on acting choices.
- The audition begins the minute you arrive on site, not when you introduce yourself.
- Greet the auditors when you walk in the door.
- Treat the pianist with care and respect—he or she is your partner in an audition.
- Be sure to be thorough with the accompanist—point out tempo and key changes, give a clear starting signal, and note any jumps or repeats.
- Give a simple, concise, and clear introduction to your audition. State your name and the titles of all of your pieces clearly and slowly; nothing more is necessary. Remember the K.I.S.S. method!

- Practice your introduction and transitions as part of your audition.
- Have backup pieces prepared in case they want to hear something different.
- Hook them in the first 30 seconds of your audition.
- Always *act* the song.
- Establish an imaginary scene partner for every piece, and stay open and visible.
- Be certain all movement (pacing, sitting, dancing, etc.) is character driven.
- Say "yes" to any direction offered to you.
- Never make excuses or apologize for your work.
- After buttoning your final piece, simply say, "Thank you," and wait a beat for a response. Then retrieve your music, thank the pianist, and leave the room gracefully.
- After the audition is done, make a journal entry and then let it go. Reward yourself for preparing and attending the audition, but don't harp on it after it's done.

④

CALLBACKS

MISSION ACCOMPLISHED

An actor's goal at an audition is always to earn a callback. Being cast is of course the greater hope, but there are too many variables involved in final casting decisions that are completely out of your control; pulling your hair out over it during your audition doesn't help at all. Just get them to want to see more of you, and you will have been successful.

You may receive notice of a callback in one of several ways. Some directors will decide on the spot if they want you to come back—some will even hand out callback sides (pieces of the script or score) at your initial audition so that you may look them over for a night before returning—another argument for not rushing out the door at the end, wouldn't you say?

Some directors will post a callback list once auditions are complete, and you will be expected to check to see if you made the list. This is most common in high schools, colleges, and large convention-style auditions such as Straw Hats, SETC (Southeastern Theatre Conference), or UPTA (Unified Professional Theatre Auditions). The other possibility is that you will actually receive a phone call from the director or the stage manager asking you to come back in.

However you are invited to attend the callbacks, you will likely have very little time to prepare. It would be wise, then, to gather as much information as possible when you are asked to return. If you are offered a callback in person or over the phone, be certain to ask what the callback will entail: Will there be dancing? Would they like you to prepare any other selections? Are there sides from the show available to peruse? Some of these questions may already be answered for you without you having to ask, but you are responsible for keeping a checklist of such pertinent information. To that end, I suggest you invest in a journal to keep a record of audition information. I'll talk more about the various important uses of a journal later, but the first is keeping track of any information transmitted regarding the callback. You don't want to show up unprepared.

If your name is posted on a list, all of the necessary details of the callback will usually be outlined on the call-board as well. Be sure to read carefully so you know what to prepare for the following day.

Once you have all the information available regarding the callback, you must put what little time you have into doing as much preparation as possible. If you haven't done so already, try to familiarize yourself with the libretto and music of the show you're going in for. Focus on the specific character or characters for which you are being considered so that you are able to make some intelligent acting choices when you read or sing. Don't lose face by asking the director to explain to you who your character is and what the character wants, when that information was readily available to you. Instead, *show the director that you did your homework*.

If they have given you sides, do your best to become very familiar with them—if possible, recruit a buddy to read through them with you. By no means are you ever expected or required to memorize the sides. Doing so demonstrates an obvious commitment to the project, but I've never known of casting choices hinging on such a minor detail. Whether you have the time and the inclination to get off-book for a callback or not, you should *always hold the script pages in your hand*—even if you never refer to them; it's just common protocol. Too often, actors end up trying to wow a director with their memorization skills only to find that they forget the lines once they are acting opposite a partner. Think about it: no matter how much you cram, one night isn't usually enough time to know a scene by rote and be able to interact honestly with a partner. In the moment, you are bound to lose your words. You avoid a slowdown or complete stoppage of the audition if you keep the script pages nearby for quick reference.

If you are given musical cuttings for a callback, you must do your utmost to learn the tunes. If you read music, sit down at a piano and plunk it out; if not, try to find someone who can do it for you (perhaps your vocal coach). As a last resort, you may refer to the original cast recording, but I've already warned you about this pitfall, so use it sparingly. If you are going in for a new musical, a cast recording may not even be available.

Frequently, musical sides will be taught at the callback. In these cases, the musical director will play through the music and answer questions before individuals are asked to sing for the director, but you must not rely on this crutch. Take it upon yourself to learn the music before the audition and then use any teaching time at the actual call to review for yourself. You'll find there is a lot less pressure when you aren't struggling to hear, learn, and remember notes and rhythms on the fly. Once again, you'll be free to focus on making solid acting choices, which will set you apart from the rest of the pack. If you are forced to learn a song at the callback, ask the musical director if it's okay to tape-record the melody, so that you may step outside and review it while waiting your turn to sing for them. You'll be glad you brought that tape recorder with you.

Sometimes you will be asked to return for a second audition, but you won't be given any materials to prepare. This is often the case in the profession when casting involves a screening process. You may audition first for a casting director or her assistant, and then be asked to come back for the director, then the producers, and so on. I've seen friends go in for upwards of *seven* auditions before a decision was made!

The same is true when attending URTA (University Resident Theatre Association), the national screening for graduate training programs, and conferences such as SETC, NETC (New England Theatre Conference), Straw Hats, and others. You audition for a panel of many, and you are called in for appointments by any schools or theatre companies that are interested in you. At these appointments, they may ask you to do your audition materials once more and offer you some directorial adjustments. Or they may simply want to chat with you and get to know you.

If you are asked to come back for a second look and you are not given any sides, you may assume that they will want you to present the same audition material that you performed the first time. Furthermore, when this is the case, you should not try to reinvent yourself. Rather, make the same acting choices that you utilized to earn the callback in the first place—they obviously saw something they liked. Essentially, the "second viewing" type of callback of which I'm speaking should be handled just as you would handle a first audition. You must be prepared to present other selections if asked, and you must take directorial adjustments if any are offered. The only difference between this call and your initial audition is that you can go in confident that you already have someone behind the table who thinks you are a good match for the project.

Sometimes you may receive a callback without even auditioning. Remember when I told you that actors will audition for a project, not be right for it, and get a call from a director later on for a different show? Or perhaps a casting director saw your work in another production and wants to call you in for something he is auditioning. I always say that the best way to audition is to be seen in a show. If you find yourself in one of these situations where you are asked to come in and audition, treat it like a callback. Get all of the necessary information about what will be asked of you, and prepare with the confidence that somebody in there really wants to see you for this show.

THE CLOTHES OFT PROCLAIM . . .

Unless you are specifically called back to dance or to move, which would require you to come in specific dance attire, the general rule of thumb is to wear what you wore the first time. Believe it or not, some directors will see so many actors at an audition that you will be remembered by your outfit (*We're calling back the guy in the light blue collared shirt for "Bobby."*) You do the director and yourself a service by presenting the same look when you return.

An obvious exception to the rule is the instance when a director or casting director asks you to dress a specific way or to style your hair differently for the callback. Barring such a request from the auditors, it is important to keep in mind that they called you in because they liked what they saw the first time. It may have been your acting, your singing, or your looks (hopefully, all of the above!), but you may never know what interested them about you. Any unsolicited change in your overall presentation may skew their opinion of you and they may decide you aren't what they were seeking.

As is the case with any audition you attend, it's never a bad idea to have dance clothes and a change of shoes with you, just in case. You should try to anticipate any possibility at a callback.

IT'S JUST A JUMP TO THE LEFT

The portion of the audition I have not yet addressed is the dance component. Perhaps this is owing to the fact that I myself am a horrid dancer who fears and loathes learning choreography. Or possibly I have dedicated little time to a part of the audition for which you can't much prepare in advance. That said, I can offer some practical advice for the dance call. It applies to the profession as well as to college auditions.

The most obvious advantage you can give yourself in a dance audition is training. Back when I auditioned for musical theatre programs, finding boys who could dance was a rarity, so I was able to slip through the cracks with both of my left feet. Now, however, the competition has grown tenfold. Even men with some dance experience often find themselves turned away by top programs. I specify males because unfortunately the competition has always been and will likely always be stiffer for females. Due to sheer numbers and gender imbalance, girls must usually meet higher expectations to be recruited. The sad part is that in the industry, the majority of roles in plays and musicals tend to be written for men as well. Women in show business will always have more of an uphill battle.

For both genders, experience offers you a decided advantage. Therefore, any chance you have to take ballet, jazz, tap, modern, or social dance classes in your school or community will be a great benefit to you. Additionally, performing in musicals that require dancing will be helpful; any opportunity you can take to practice learning, integrating, and repeating choreography will serve you well in the future. At the very least, you must be able to listen attentively, find the rhythm, and sell the joy that dancing brings you. If it doesn't, you'd better sell the joy that *acting* like a dancer brings!

When you attend an audition with a dance component, be sure to wear appropriate attire. They will almost always allow a short break for you to change clothes between the dance call and the singing/acting auditions, so you do not usually have to do your solo pieces in a leotard or sweats. Ideally, you should wear real dance clothes; however, if you don't own any, wear something comfortable yet formfitting that allows the lines and contours of your body to be observed while in motion. *Do not wear jeans and do not dance in socks or sneakers.* If you are serious about a career in musical theatre, you'll need to invest in ballet and jazz shoes, so you might as well get them before you start auditioning. Women should own character shoes with heels as well as flats and have both options available at a dance call.

Once the choreographer begins teaching the combinations, pay close attention to detail, making sure you are in a position to see her entire body clearly. If you have specific questions or you find yourself lost, raise your hand and politely ask for clarification or repetition. I've never known even the strictest dance instructor to refuse repeating steps for a pupil who finds himself challenged (and believe me, I've known some strict dance instructors, and I have been very challenged!). Whatever you do, be sure not to break off into conversations with the people around you—asking or answering combination questions, complaining about how hard the dance is, or celebrating its simplicity. There is no quicker way to enrage the choreographer and find yourself on the do-not-cast list. If you need help, ask the figure of authority. If someone around you needs help, suggest they do the same.

No matter how impossible you think the combination is, it is important to maintain a game face and a level head. They are likely to challenge candidates to see how quickly you pick up steps and how much you can absorb, but they rarely expect you to be able to nail every combination perfectly. If you can present an illusion of confidence—acting your way through the dance audition—then you will be fine. *If you forget a step, just keep moving and try to find your way back to the choreography.* And beware of watching the people who are dancing around you as you audition. If you're following them, they are likely to steer you wrong. Retain what you can and try to enjoy repeating it.

I want to let you in on one other little secret I've learned about dance auditions. Whereas acting and singing are auditory skills—I can listen to you as I bury my head in my pad and make notes—dance is a purely visual communication. If I am not looking directly at you, I miss a part of your performance. Further, in a dance audition you usually do not perform alone: You'll likely be in a group of two or more others dancing beside you. This means that the focus will be divided among yourself and your cohorts.

Where am I going with all of this? Well, even the most experienced dancers on occasion will make mistakes in a combination; it's not rare and it's not surprising. Inexperienced performers, however, compound their errors by telegraphing them after the fact. We've all done it—missed a step or tripped, and then laughed, froze, said "oops," or any number of other acknowledgements of our flawed performance.

Do you see how reacting to your own little gaffes only increases the odds that they will be noticed? There's a very strong possibility that they weren't even looking at you when you turned right instead of left, but you made sure to draw their attention to your mistake by laughing and shaking your head. Even if your trip or your fall out of a pirouette turn catches their eyes, recovery is part of what they are judging you on. So either way, it behooves you to continue dancing and fight your way through it when the going gets rough. You'll slip through the cracks more often than you might expect. I've seen many actors have successful auditions during which they forgot all or most of the choreography that was taught. They got cast because of their ability to continue moving improvisationally while staying in character, rather than simply standing still and looking lost.

WHO COULD ASK FOR ANYTHING MORE?

Throughout this book, I have no doubt exhausted you with my repetition of the mantra: *The goal of an audition is to get a callback*. I won't cease drilling that notion into your head—close the book and it's on the cover! But now, here we are discussing how to properly handle a callback and we have not paused to address the issue of what the actor's goal should be once she gets a callback. I mean, if you've come this far, you successfully achieved your initial objective, so what now?

You may say, "Duh, Flom. The goal of a callback is to get a job offer." And while I agree that being cast would be wonderful, I would also suggest that you may find that making it your objective will lead to a great deal of disappointment. I hate to be cynical, but let's face it, you're going to audition a lot more often than you'll be cast; it's just a statistical fact. And the more a person fails to achieve personal career goals, the more likely she is to give up and change careers. Thus it follows: if you set your mind on getting work every time you audition, you'll encounter disappointment with a high frequency, and eventually you will give up. If, however, you make it your goal at each and every callback you attend to (1) have fun and (2) let them see you at your best, you will stand a much greater chance of achieving a 100% success rate. You will have more control. What's more, focusing on a positively attainable objective will make you more desirable to directors, and you will probably find yourself fielding more job offers this way.

It may sound as though I'm quibbling over subtle semantics, but I really believe that naming a realistic goal over which you are capable of asserting your control is extremely empowering. You'll perform with confidence once you stop trying to please the director and start making every audition an opportunity to be the best performer you can be. You won't always get the part, but you'll be able to walk away feeling good about what you showed the auditors.

I can't count the number of times I've heard of actors being passed over at one audition because they weren't right for the part, only to be called in later for a different project on the merit of their earlier showing. You can never know exactly what they're looking for; you can only show them what you have to offer and let them decide. Most directors you audition for will be casting one specific project with their next two future productions already in the back of their minds. Plus, other people in the audition room might be casting other shows as well. You never know what one good, yet seemingly unsuccessful, audition will yield later on.

BUT I PLAY ONE ON TV

As I stated earlier, you must offer a positive response to directorial adjustments in an audition. The reply "Yes, I can do that" is one you should practice and be ready to use when asked to approach a piece differently. That said, you must be careful not to say it if it isn't true.

For example, an actor goes in for a replacement call in *Wicked*. She sings well and impresses the casting director enough to earn a second audition. At the callback, it turns out that they are looking for someone with acrobatic and tumbling skills. The actor, eager to be considered for a big Broadway gig, nods enthusiastically when asked if she has any gymnastic abilities. Unfortunately, the only tumbling she's ever done has been somersaults in preschool. Now that actor has painted herself into a corner, and there is really no easy way for her to save face. You cannot always be what they need. You must remember to be honest with the director and with yourself.

On the other hand, there are times when you should allow yourself to ride on your acting skills. When I was back in my performing days, I was the least confident dancer you could have ever met. In spite of my four years of BFA training, I avoided dance calls like the plague. I hated having to learn choreography; however, if I ever went in for a singing audition and was asked if I danced, my answer was always, "Sure." Why did I do that? Because my very basic knowledge of ballet, jazz, and tap, combined with my acting abilities, made me very capable at faking my way through most dance calls. Sure, I didn't have great extension or pointed toes, nor could I always keep up with all the steps; but I always sold it. I sold it by having fun and *acting* like a dancer. If they were looking to fill a serious dance role, I obviously did not stand a chance at getting the part; but if they needed an actor who could move, that was perfectly achievable for me.

The bottom line is this: if they ask about skills that you absolutely do not possess (and cannot fake), you must be honest and tell them you can't do it. If, however, it may be possible to look good trying, then go for it, as long as you can appear confident. I have a friend who once went in for a production of *A Little Night Music* (Sondheim). He was perfect for the role of Henrik, the brooding young son, except for the fact that the musical requires Henrik to play the cello on stage. The character accompanies himself in his big

Act 1 solo, "Later." But my friend had never played a cello in his life. When asked if he could play, my friend smiled and said, "You bet." He earned himself a callback, and two days later he had learned how to muddle his way through "Later" enough to get the part. I wouldn't recommend this kind of risk to everyone, but he knew that he was musical enough to show them what they needed to hear, and so he went for it. That kind of confidence alone can be worthy of a job.

AND THAT BRINGS US BACK TO . . .

The unique thing about being an actor (as if there were only one unique thing about being an actor!) is that even when you have a job, you're always looking for work. Broadway performers do most of their shows in the evening. During their daytime off-hours, they can often be found auditioning. It's even the same with acting schools—once you get in, you'll still be required to audition every time a show is being cast. Auditioning *is* the job of an actor. If you are ready to commit your life to the art of performing, you had better embrace the idea of auditioning. You had better be prepared to put yourself on display and to be judged, and you must learn not to take the judgment personally. Moreover, you had better take stock of what you can and cannot control and invest your time in learning to master factors that are within your command rather than beating yourself up over those that are not.

Continue to study voice and dance, even when you are out of school. Keep your body in optimum physical condition. Read and see plays as often as possible to discover new material for your repertoire. And when you attend auditions, be grateful for the opportunity to be seen performing. You will find your overall mental health enhanced greatly by maintaining a proper, positive outlook. You will also learn that people who truly love their jobs do better at them: Love to audition.

SECRET AGENT MAN

Many young actors ask me to explain agents and casting directors—what they do and the differences between them. So here's a very brief crash course on these all-important friends of your career.

An agent is an industry insider who has the power to open doors for actors. Producers and casting directors send out "breakdowns," or specifics about an audition, to agents; the agents then submit their clients who are appropriate for that particular call. Agents can get actors access to auditions that they would never otherwise have on their own. An agency may represent anywhere from 15 to 50 performers, depending on the size of the office and the scope of its operation. They may deal in theatre, film, television, or all three. When an agent takes an actor on as a client, he will frequently give the actor a modest amount of career management advice, including what to wear, which headshot is right, and what material to use for auditions. The agent will often seek out feedback for the client after an audition as well, in order to help the actor improve. And of course, the agent makes money when the actor makes money: the standard rate is 10 percent of the actor's paycheck. So if you sign with a good agency, they will work hard for you.

Getting signed with an agent can prove to be quite enigmatic. I wish there were a simple cut-and-dry way to go about doing so, but unfortunately no formula exists. Some colleges will showcase their graduating class to agents as their first exposure, after which the actors may choose to follow up and ask for a formal audition. Some actors find representation when an agent sees them in a production. And sometimes a friend who is signed with an agency may recommend you to them, thus getting you in the door. Those are really the only common ways I know of to get yourself an agent. Unfortunately, sending an unsolicited letter of interest without having some introduction or common connection to the agency does not usually tend to pan out.

The casting director works on the other side of the table. He is hired by a producer or theatre company essentially to "weed out" actors and dig for appropriate talent to show the director of a production. When a casting director is hired, he must understand the needs of the show as seen through the director's vision. He will then either send a breakdown to agents or place a public advertisement in the trade papers and hold open auditions. Sometimes casting directors who have a previous relationship with certain actors will call them directly and ask them to come in for a project that they feel would be a good match. Thus, it's not a bad idea to have casting directors who like you.

Once you go through an initial screening with the casting director, if she is interested in you for the project, she will ask you to come back in for the artistic staff of the production, including the director, the producers, the writers, the choreographer, and so on. So while the casting director generally does not have final say in who gets hired, she can give you a free pass right to the final cut, where the director or the producer ultimately chooses who is cast.

Agents and casting directors tend to have a "you scratch my back, I'll scratch yours" relationship. The casting director needs the agent to submit good quality actors, and the agent needs the casting director to employ his clients. Needless to say, finding yourself in good stead with any of these people is to your benefit. I've even heard of the occasional situation in which an unrepresented actor who has had some great auditions for a casting director gets recommended by that person to a big agency. Again, your reputation as a professional will mean everything out there in the real world.

SUMMARY

- Be sure to ask questions and gather all the information when you receive a callback.
- Whether you memorize or not, always hold the script pages in your hand during a callback.
- Do your best to learn on your own any music handed out for callbacks.
- Unless otherwise instructed, wear the same clothes to the callback that you wore to the initial audition.
- Unless otherwise instructed, make the same acting and vocal choices at the callback that you made at the initial audition.
- Bring dance clothes and dance shoes to every musical audition you attend. Do not wear jeans and do not dance in socks or street sneakers.
- If you forget a step in the dance combination, keep moving and try to find your way back, always acting through the entire process.
- Don't focus on trying to get the job. Instead, concentrate on having fun and offering them your best performance at every audition.
- If asked to make an adjustment, say yes. If asked whether you possess a skill which you do not possess (and cannot fake), say no.
- Love to audition!

5

AUDITIONING FOR COLLEGES

A note to readers: this chapter is specifically intended to address the needs of high school students making the transition to college training programs. Although I believe it is interesting and informative even for those who are beyond college auditions, you may certainly feel free to skip over this unit and continue with chapter 6: Job Offers.

One of the most exciting and intriguing aspects of my background has been recruiting for the musical theatre programs at Penn State and Shenandoah Conservatory. Both universities offer competitive, individualized training grounds, and their reputations attract hundreds of prospective young actors from all over the country every year. Consequently, I have seen some of the best, some of the worst, and some of the most misguided high school performers present themselves as candidates.

Furthermore, I often offer my services to hopeful teens seeking guidance and mentoring through the stressful process of entrance auditions. I have advised on song and monologue choices and I have coached acting. And through my experience, I have come to understand the college screening process as a singular, unique process, similar in many ways to "real world" auditions, but at the same time an art in itself.

I therefore thought it useful to dedicate a unit of this book to the specific challenges of training program auditions. I offer you, the high school junior or senior, this chapter with the assumption that you have first read the preceding sections of the book, as the information I have laid out thus far will be useful in a college setting.

WHAT MUST I DO?

The first trick to solving college auditions is to understand their purpose. Unlike casting, where you are expected to already possess the "tools" and to fulfill the description of a particular character, institutions do not generally require you to fit a specific mold. It is the raison d'être of a program to help shape you and hone your talents, to endow you with the proverbial craft to accompany your artistry.

Thus, the idea that a student must be a polished "triple threat" to earn consideration from a decent school is a fallacy. A good program seeks trainable candidates: young men and women who possess the potential to grow and blossom into successful artists under four years of tutelage. For, what would a teacher have to offer the complete, accomplished performer? How can that student truly be a *student*?

What you must present to college instructors is an enthusiastic, pliable piece of high-quality clay that they can sculpt; a sapling that, under their care and tending, will bear glorious fruit. In short, to dispense with lofty metaphors, you need to display the basic fundamentals of a performer, the capability of tremendous growth, and the unquestionable desire to achieve that growth. A great personality certainly helps as well.

Don't get me wrong, if you can't carry a tune or speak coherently, there might not be a program in the country that will accept you, but you do not have to be Gregory Hines. Generally, if you are proficient in at least one area (acting, singing, dancing), capable in a second, and teachable in the third, you should have options available to you.

Once you have spent some much-needed time reflecting on your ambitions and have decided you are prepared to commit to the arduous life of the theatre professional, you must then convince your chosen auditors that you are up to the task. You do so by preparing fully and displaying professionalism beyond your years, as I have detailed throughout this book. The girl who comes in with two random cuttings from *The Ordinary Soprano's Anthology* and a gut-wrenching tale of anorexia and bulimia from *The Book of Pointless Monologues for Young People* is quickly forgotten; but the girl who has chosen contrasting, well-considered songs that display acting range *and* vocal ability, along with an *age-appropriate* monologue from a play she would be suitable for, distinguishes herself. (See the appendix for suggested source material for young actors.)

Although it is understood that you have not yet been taught all of the ins and outs of auditioning well, you can really stand out and impress college panels by exceeding expectations with your preparedness. Having a book of well-rehearsed songs—even a small selection—organized neatly in a binder; dealing appropriately with the accompanist; introducing yourself confidently and delivering a poised, if imperfect, performance; and conveying a sincere love for what you do—these aspects will win you as much interest and respect as a terrific belt voice or a triple pirouette.

Few college auditions will require your music to be tape-recorded—most will provide an accompanist. Unless otherwise specified, be prepared to work with the school's pianist. Do not bring a parent to play for your audition. Colleges are often turned off by overinvolved stage parents who wish to walk their child through everything and micromanage. A parent should be supportive . . . outside of the audition room.

Dress nicely in clothes that make you look and feel your best and show them what you have to offer. Most young people don't tend to feel at home in jackets and ties, so there's no need to bring that sort of formality to your college auditions. Nice casual is usually preferable to overly dressy. Make strong acting choices, just as I suggested in dealing with professional castings. And likewise, be flexible and open to adjustments. My colleagues and I almost always offer some direction to students who interest us. For example, an actor might be asked to try the song again with a live scene partner to work off of, or he might be told to try operating from a different point of view or emotional state. Again, we are looking to discover whether a prospective trainee will accept instruction and take risks. Occasionally, you may also be asked if you have an alternative song selection, just like in a professional audition.

Staying the Course

The decision to attend a professional training program for acting or for musical theatre is a serious matter and should be reflected upon before making a commitment. I say this to you because I have noticed more and more often that students seem to get distracted during their school years. If they are in close enough proximity to a city—particularly New York—they will go off to attend open casting calls for shows that are in their age and type range, such as *Spring Awakening*, which requires a particularly youthful cast. One such student of mine was recently offered a contract in the first national tour of that very production.

While it is wonderful for someone so young and fresh to walk off with a national tour contract before even moving to New York and "paying his dues," as it were, it is also a risky move. Once that tour is over, if the student does not move directly to the Broadway company of that show, he will be left without a degree and, more importantly, without being completely trained. Although his rawness was ideal for *Spring Awakening*, he may not be suited for the majority of professional work that is available when he finishes his tour. Furthermore, he is now stuck with his Equity union card, and he can only audition for union productions for which he'll be competing with older, more seasoned performers.

That young actor also finds himself without agent representation, since he was cast out of an open cattle call. Although some would argue that having an agent is not an essential, it certainly would be a big help to a young, inexperienced actor with no real knowledge of how to navigate his way through the business. That young man has made a decision to abandon his training and take advantage of a wonderfully exciting opportunity that will likely employ him for one year; however, he is not considering the long-term big picture.

Don't get me wrong—I'm not saying his career will be over the minute he returns from his tour. I have another former student who took a Broadway gig after his sophomore year. When that show closed, he returned to school for two years and now is back in New York and back on Broadway. But I must emphasize how exceedingly rare such instances are. You need to remember why you chose to go to school in the first place, and you need to trust that there will be just as many exciting audition opportunities available to you after you finish school as there are now. New York will always be there!

Some schools will not allow students to attend outside auditions, period. If you feel as though the draw to get out and work will be too strong for you, then consider attending a two-year certificate program in the city, such as AMDA or The Neighborhood Playhouse. But realize that if you commit to a four-year institution, it will take all your concentration and dedication to get the most out of your training experience.

The best high school audition I ever saw was a young girl named Shaina—I still remember her name, even though she chose to study elsewhere. This girl came in and danced quite adequately, as I recall, though nothing particularly stand-out. She sang well—an obviously trained (and trainable) voice—but she wasn't the greatest singer any of us had ever heard. Then she began her monologue. Within 10 seconds, it was obvious that she had chosen this supposed "comedic" performance piece from a book of standard, contentless monologues. It was the alternative to the melodramatic tear-jerker: the hilarious, slay-em-in-the-aisles routine. It had no heart, no substance, and it offered no indication of any acting ability.

I asked Shaina to stop about 30 seconds into the piece. "Do you have anything else prepared?" I asked her. Most 18-year-olds (heck, most adults!) would panic and freeze, certain that they had failed. But not this girl. She paused for an instant to catch her breath and step out of "performance mode," and she flashed us a knowing smile; a smile that said "I know exactly why you're asking me to show you something different."

She asked if *Laramie Project* would be a better choice, and with our assent she hesitated not a moment before grabbing a chair, sitting, and launching into the greatest delivery of that overdone monologue that I had ever seen. She didn't miss a single beat, transitioning seamlessly from over-the-top shtick to real and focused dramatic acting.

When she was finished, I asked her if she felt the second piece served her better than the first, and we shared a good laugh at her obvious triumph. In a brief, two-minute span, this young girl showed us her talent, her confidence, her preparation, her intelligence, and above all her personality. Undeniably, we—and I suspect any other school that saw her—wanted to work with her.

That's the key, my friends: make them *want* to work with you.

TELL US ABOUT YOURSELF . . .

Since we have already discussed handling the dance call in the previous chapter, we'll move on to the last segment of a college entrance audition: the interview. Some colleges will talk with every candidate, while others, in the interest of time, will only sit down with those whom they are seriously interested in recruiting. When I auditioned as an incoming student for Penn State, everyone had an interview; however, now that they attract the overwhelming numbers of a top-tier training school, they tend to release a good deal of the young men and women after their performance portion is complete, in order to dedicate more time to becoming acquainted with their top prospects.

And that is exactly the purpose behind the interview: getting to know you as a person, outside of your performance. *It is essential, then, that you not try to put on any sort of artificial display when you meet with the panel.* You've already shown them your acting abilities; now you need to share your humanity. The successful candidate is one who can be serious and personable, tenacious and level-headed, and confident and humble. Before you attend a college audition, ask yourself why you want to study musical theatre and why you'd like to do it at that particular institution. These are likely the first questions they'll ask you. You don't want to sound too rehearsed and robotic, but you don't want to be caught off-guard stammering, either. Giving some prior consideration to this, and similar questions, will not only prepare you well for the interview, but it will also help you to better identify what you desire in a program and in life.

When I first began recruiting for the college, I asked the head of the program why we even bothered with interviews. They all seemed exactly the same to me. Nine out of ten went just like this:

"Well, I started performing when I was five. I've *always* wanted to be an actor. I live for the thrill of applause. I know someday I'll make it on Broadway. I just *have* to do it . . . "

So what is it that we glean from the same tired story over and over? His answer: It's the one in ten who tells a different story. It didn't take me long to see what he meant.

My now-dear friend Morgan was a nontraditional candidate for the program at Penn State. She was several years older than the incoming class, as she had taken some time off to work after high school. She knew that musicals were her one true passion—that's prerequisite for a life in this business—and she researched all of her options for training. At a particular convention in New Mexico, where she lived, she met Mary Saunders, the Penn State voice instructor. Something drew Morgan to her and they just clicked as teacher and student.

Morgan began to read about the rest of the program at Penn State, and she decided that it was the perfect match for her. She visited, attended classes, and confirmed her belief that "Happy Valley" was where she belonged. She also discovered that an out-of-state school was unaffordable, an impossible dream (pardon the musical theatre reference) without scholarships and financial aid, for which she might not qualify.

But she was undeterred by economic obstacles. Morgan moved in with her sister in Philadelphia and waited tables for a year while she earned legal residency status to qualify for in-state tuition rates. She just *had* to go to Penn State, and she would go to any lengths to get there.

When she finally came to audition for us, she was not the best, most exciting performer in the pack. She had raw vocal abilities and little dance training, and she was aware of her shortcomings. In her interview, she related her story of determination, and she told us she wanted Penn State to make her a better dancer, a better singer, a better actor. She said she had chosen this school because she felt she could find her full potential with the individualized training being offered, and she asserted her absolute commitment to work hard to achieve the best results possible.

I don't need to tell you that the interview secured Morgan's place in the incoming BFA class. In two minutes, this girl showed more grit, more candor, and more personality than anyone else I have ever seen in a college interview. And it really paid off for her.

Now, that's not to say that you need to have a tale of uphill, against-all-odds battles to have a successful interview. And it certainly doesn't mean that taking a year off to earn residency in the school's state will get you in; Morgan took a huge risk with that move. But you do need to find your unique voice and show them that you are special and worthy of their attention. Spending some time reflecting on these "why" questions will help you to better know yourself, and self-awareness will get you far in life. Not to mention, a keen sense of self is both very appealing and fairly unusual in prospective college students.

There's not much else you can do to prepare for the interview. They may ask any number of assorted questions, which you'll have to answer off the cuff. They may want to talk about your audition performance. When I auditioned for NYU, the man sat me down and asked how I thought I did—tell me that's not a no-win situation! But whatever they throw at you, they just want you to be yourself. *Listen attentively, make eye contact, and respond affably, and you will do well.*

Assuming you've done your research and read up on a program before going to your audition, you may find that you have some questions for them as well. The interviewers will usually ask if you have any questions, and you should not be shy to speak up if you do. Consider such concerns as the following:

- How many general education credits will you need to graduate?
- What merit-based scholarships might be available to you?
- What is the first-year campus living experience like?
- Will you be allowed (or required) to audition for productions in the first year?
- Does this school have a network of alumni in New York, Chicago, and Los Angeles?

You may need this information when making your final choice of schools, plus it's an opportunity to continue conversing with the auditors. Don't overlook the fact that you are interviewing them just as much as they are you. They are shopping for students, but you are shopping for a suitable training program all the same. When you begin to receive acceptance letters and you must decide where your tuition dollars are to go, you'll want to make the most informed decision possible. So why not engage the professors in a little Q and A yourself and see how well they respond to your queries?

WHERE AM I GOING?

The selection of a college training program is a highly personal, life-shaping decision that should not be taken lightly. You must do your own research and try to learn what all the different schools have to offer before you begin applying and auditioning. Although all of your friends may tell you that school A is the place to go if you want to make it as an actor, you may find that school B speaks more to your own interests. For instance, do you want a conservatory, where every hour of the day will be dedicated to the performing arts, or are you better off at a liberal arts university, where you'll receive a broader, more well-rounded education? These are considerations you'll have to ponder as you begin your college search.

Get a sense of what you're looking for before you begin auditioning. Then, be sure to visit all of your possible schools throughout the audition/decision process. Sit in on classes and attend departmental productions when possible to get a sense of the kind of work they do. Talk to current students and find out what they like and dislike about their program. They're usually more than willing to give you the inside scoop. And once you start receiving acceptance letters, you will be prepared to make an informed choice.

I had a dream school in mind for many years. As the end of high school approached, I *knew* I was destined to go there. Yet, when I went to visit and audition, the school wasn't what I had envisioned at all. The environment was less than welcoming, and the experience fell far short of the college's reputation. Then I went to look at a university that barely had a reputation at all; its BFA program was only in its second year of existence. It was a far cry from what I *thought* I needed, but on my visit I discovered that it offered everything I could ever want. Had I not gone to visit my college options, I would never have chosen to attend Penn State, and some of the best years of my life would have surely been written very differently.

By no means am I trying to say that my alma mater is the best one out there, but it was the best one for me. You need to get out there and experience these campuses first-hand and find the one that feels like home to *you*. Only then will you be making the best possible decision for your college years.

The following list may be helpful to you if you are starting from scratch with no information. These are just some of the schools that offer training programs in musical theatre. This is by no means a complete list—it is simply a collection of some of the more well-known schools regionally. It may help you to get started on your search.

Boston Conservatory (Boston, Massachusetts)
New York University (New York, New York)
Carnegie Mellon University (Pittsburgh, Pennsylvania)
Northwestern University (Chicago, Illinois)
Cincinnati Conservatory (Cincinnati, Ohio)
Penn State University (State College, Pennsylvania)
Elon University (Elon, North Carolina)
Roosevelt University (Chicago, Illinois)
Emerson College (Boston, Massachusetts)
Shenandoah Conservatory (Winchester, Virginia)
Florida State University (Tallahassee, Florida)
SUNY Fredonia (Fredonia, New York)
Ithaca College (Ithaca, New York)
Syracuse University (Syracuse, New York)
James Madison University (Harrisonburg, Virginia)
University of the Arts (Philadelphia, PA)
University of Miami (Miami, Florida)
Webster University (St. Louis, Missouri)
University of Michigan (Ann Arbor, Michigan)
Wright State University (Dayton, Ohio)

SUMMARY

- Colleges are looking for trainable candidates, not polished triple threats.
- You can set yourself apart from the multitudes of average students by being thoroughly prepared, choosing age-appropriate pieces, and making solid acting choices for each audition piece.

- Do not bring a parent to accompany your audition.
- Be yourself in the interview—don't try to "act" your way through it.
- Avoid cliché responses, such as "I've always wanted to be on Broadway," or "I do it because I love the rush of applause."
- Research the schools you are auditioning for, and ask questions of them in your interview, so that you have all the information needed to make an informed decision.
- Visit colleges and sit in on classes and productions to determine the best fit for your individual training needs.

JOB OFFERS

WHAT TO DO, WHAT TO SAY

Most audition books tend to leave you on your own once you complete the callback; some don't even extend beyond the initial call. But I really believe that some discussion on what to do after you have been seen will be valuable. After all, fielding offers is as much a part of the game as answering casting calls. Realistically, you will not be able to (nor will you necessarily want to) take every job you are offered. So in this chapter, we will examine several factors to consider once the proverbial ball is in your court.

Back in the early pages of this book, I advised you to read casting notices carefully and to consider whether you would want a particular job before going in for an audition. But it is not always possible to make this determination before an offer is made. Even a thorough casting ad will lack certain details that you will only discover once you begin to negotiate with the producers.

Every professional actor has stories of being burned by bad project choices in his career. The greener you are, the more likely you'll be to accept any role just for the credit and the exposure. You will find that experience educates in these matters. But you can greatly reduce the risk of making unhappy commitments if you take the time to thoroughly consider the circumstances at hand and to be a little selective when possible.

Begin by gathering as much information as possible when a role is offered to you. Find out exactly how much it pays, how long it runs, how often
it rehearses, where you are expected to be and when and how you'll get
there, and where you'll stay. Don't be afraid to ask a lot of questions when
you first get that call from a theatre. And once you have obtained all of the
details, you simply *must* say, *"Let me think about it and call you back."*

Too many actors, excited just to receive an offer, wind up stuck in a
miserable project because they said yes without looking at the big picture.
You have every right to take some time to consider an offer before getting
on board. Don't allow yourself to get swept away and make a rash decision.
Most directors and producers will allow you 24 hours *at the very least* to
ponder their offer. They will respect you for taking the time to be certain
you can commit to the project before rushing in.

FOR YOUR CONSIDERATION

When a job opportunity comes your way, there are many factors that can
aid in your decision-making process. Determining whether a job is worth
the overall commitment comprises several questions, the answers to which
may sway you strongly toward or away from accepting work. The following
is a checklist of sorts that you should utilize when fielding an offer.

How long will the production require your dedication?
Will you be tied up in rehearsals and/or workshops for two months, followed by a nine-month run? Or the opposite: Will you be putting your life
(and your day job) on hold to take a gig that rehearses for a week, runs
for two weeks, then leaves you unemployed once more? There is no right
answer to help you deal with this question—only what is right for you. Just
be certain you understand what you are being asked to do before you agree
to it.

Where is the gig?
For a New York actor, accepting a role with a small professional theatre
in North Jersey is vastly different than taking the same role in Birmingham,
Alabama. Can you afford to be away from the city for the length of the contract? Will anybody see your work if you travel to distant places? Be sure
to examine and weigh all of the trade-offs involved in leaving your home
to take a job. Is housing and travel included, or will you need to pay out of
pocket in order to take the work? Many young actors look for opportunities

to join nonunion national tours or even cruise lines after school to travel and save up money while living rent free. Is this something you want to do, or are you more interested in planting roots?

Can you afford to accept the job?

The sad truth is, much of the acting work that's out there will pay you little to no money. community theatre, for instance, almost never pays. Frequently, taking a job must be considered an investment in your overall career; for example, the actor who does summer stock for $250 a week because it expands the résumé and keeps him in practice. Usually, the determining factors in whether you can financially justify taking a job are the above-mentioned commitment of time and location. If you feel that they are not paying enough money to get you to go, why not try negotiating for more? The worst thing they can say is no, and then you decide if you are willing to take what is on the table. But if they really want you, they may be willing to offer more money if you tell them you cannot work for their original figure.

I find that the best way to approach the issue of money is to get all the information on the initial call and ask for a few days to consider the offer. During this time, ask yourself how much money you would realistically need to take this job and still be able to pay your bills. Don't overshoot the mark (if their offer is $350 per week, don't ask for $1,200), but don't sell yourself short either ($375 isn't much of a negotiation). When you call them back, you tell them how interested you are in working with them and how grateful you are for the offer; however, at this point in time it's a real stretch for you financially. Ask if the salary is negotiable. At this point, they may say one of three things: "No it's not," in which case, you need to be prepared to accept or reject their offer; "How much did you have in mind?" in which case, you tell them your figure; or "We can give you X dollars more," after which you either continue to negotiate or you make a final decision. I see too many actors get into tough financial crunches because they don't treat themselves like a *business* and they make poor *business* choices. Remember, the name of this thing is show *business*.

If a theatre is unwilling to be flexible on salary, you might also ask for other accommodations in your contract to make it worth your while, such as transportation/airfare to the gig, a rental car, free housing, a meal stipend, your own room, and so on. Again, don't be so thankful for a job offer that you are willing to accept terrible conditions and a large financial hit to take work.

And speaking of contracts: when working in professional theatre, there will always be a contract. In amateur theatre, there is no pay involved, so everything is verbal. But if you are working in stock, regional, Off-Broadway, touring theatre, cruise ships, or any venue that is going to pay you for your work, you must insist that you get everything in writing. It is the only protection you have as an actor, especially if you don't belong to the union. A verbal acceptance of a job with certain conditions attached is a fine agreement for starters, but if you start working on a job before getting a signed contract from the producer or company, there is no telling what might happen during the process. Most theatres will send you a contract without your having to ask for it. When you receive a contract, read carefully and make sure you understand everything completely. Also, make sure that the wording reflects anything you negotiated or were promised. Remember: if it's not in writing, it's not binding. Protect yourself. You are a business, not a pawn.

What will you be giving up?

So, you have a really great full-time day job with benefits. They even allow you to take an extended lunch when there is a great audition going on. You're making enough to live comfortably in the city while many of your friends are struggling or moving away. *But are you doing what you came to do?* I pose this question to you because I had to answer it for myself some years back, and I've seen almost all of my actor friends face it as well.

There comes a time (or possibly several times) when you will be required to sacrifice something—perhaps even another acting job—in order to accept a role. It can be a frightening proposition, particularly when the offer you are considering has high artistic value but low financial reward. And so I say that you must ask yourself if you are doing what you came to do. Can you possibly survive without the cushy day job so as to move in the direction of your career ambitions?

You'll need to weigh the situation carefully before you can assess whether it's worth the risk. Only you can judge in a given circumstance what is best for you. Just do your best not to burn bridges as you make these types of decisions. I'm speaking now to the actor who is already involved in one production when another, more exciting offer comes along. In such an instance, you must tread lightly and truly reflect on whether the second job is worth walking out on the current one. It may depend on how far into the first project you have gone. Just remember that this is a very small community, and you are only as good as your reputation. Will you be damaging your future if you walk away from a commitment in your present? In these situations, actors will often help find their own replacement to save the production staff time and money.

What will you gain?

The advice given to me when I was preparing to go out into the profession was to consider three factors in a job offer: Is the pay good? Is this a role that I really should have on my résumé? Is this a director or a theatre that I really should have on my résumé? If you answer yes to two out of the three, then you should take the job for sure. If you only answer yes to one or none, then you need to seriously consider if it's worth it.

Think about what kind of exposure a gig may offer as well. Being seen performing in a production is as good a way of being cast in the future as auditioning is. Sometimes you may be offered a minor role or even an understudy job, but it will be worthwhile because a star is involved in the project. Again, think about how any particular job will look on your résumé.

Is it a union job?

This question is obviously meant for nonunion performers. I see a great deal of young actors jump at any opportunity for work that would entail joining Actors' Equity. I urge you to use caution when these offers come your way. An Equity membership is not a golden key that will unlock the door to a lifetime of work, contrary to popular and naïve opinion. In fact, many actors find that getting work, even work that pays, is much easier without being in the union.

Think about this: once you join Equity, you can *only* take union jobs. You'll be shutting yourself out of more than half of the work out there, for starters. You'll be competing with people who have already made a successful career in the theatre and have built up a credible résumé. If you are fresh out of college and your only professional experience is ensemble work at the Pittsburgh CLO, you'll find it difficult to get your foot in the door just to be seen at Equity auditions. And if a theatre has the option of casting you or your equally talented, nonunion counterpart, you can bet they'll go with your unaffiliated colleague and save themselves some money!

I always advise young actors to take some time to build up a list of quality credits before going Equity. It may mean passing on some potentially exciting work along the way, but it can prove extremely wise in the long term for your career. Often, taking one union job will lock an actor out of several years of other work.

Now don't get me wrong, I'm not suggesting that it's never good to go union when you're young. If you are offered an Equity contract that will employ you for a long period of time or provide you with maximum exposure, or if it's simply a great role that will truly enhance your résumé, then I say go for it. What I am saying, however, is don't run to the Jeckyll and

Hyde Restaurant or Theatreworks/USA because they give out Equity cards to all of their employees. Be careful about working for the MUNY in St. Louis or Pittsburgh CLO, where you will be required to take your Equity card just to work in the chorus. Again, you just need to think ahead and try to anticipate whether it will pay off for you in the big picture. Seek counsel from your teachers and mentors when you are faced with the union decision.

Do you want to work with this company?

Moments ago, I mentioned that reputations mean a great deal in the theatre industry. This is true not only for performers but also for directors and theatre companies. *Before you agree to accept a job, it is wise to investigate the theatre for which you would be working.* Talk to your friends and see if they can offer any thoughts or opinions about the company based upon their experience. You may find that while a gig sounds appealing on paper, it's not worth facing the horror stories that your fellow actors tell you about how seedy the housing is or how the paychecks have a knack for bouncing.

If you can avoid getting entrenched in miserable theatrical endeavors, you'll save yourself a good amount of stress and heartache. When you hear bad things about a theatre or a director, don't hesitate to graciously refuse the work if it doesn't seem worth the hassle.

Sadly, you'll find a great deal of disreputable theatres in big cities such as New York and Chicago. The desperate need to work often leads actors to settle for being treated poorly. With experience, you will learn how to avoid such unhappy situations, and you'll develop a network of fellow actors with whom you can exchange feedback, both negative and positive, regarding theatres where you have worked.

One piece of wisdom I am always quick to offer on the subject is this: beware of jobs that require you to pay to work. I'm not speaking of networking organizations such as Actors' Connection, which happens to be well reputed for attracting big agencies. Rather, I am referring to those theatres, sometimes known as "membership companies," that charge actors a fee to perform with them. It's one thing to be financially involved with helping your friends start up a theatre company; it's another thing entirely to be asked to contribute to a theatre's budget just to be cast in a play.

You should *never* pay to work; even if they tell you that you are investing in a "showcase" production. (My dear friend Melissa was taken in this way and found herself swindled out of $75.) Legitimate showcases do not require any money from the actors. Companies that charge actors to work are either scams or very low forms of community theatre. Either way, you'll do well to avoid them.

HOW COULD I WALK AWAY?

Earlier on, I spoke to you about being careful not to attend auditions for jobs you can't or won't take. I advised that it may be perceived by the director that you are wasting her time. In the event, however, that you audition for a project with every intent to accept an offer, only to discover an unavoidable conflict after they cast you, you must make every effort to save face.

Let me give you an example of such a situation. I was casting a production of *Cabaret* recently, and a young man contacted me about his interest in the role of Cliff. We arranged an audition time for him, and he came in very prepared and professional. The musical director and I agreed that he would be a very competent choice, and I called him two days later to offer him the part.

When he returned my call later that day, he explained that he had also auditioned for a production of *City of Angels* at a prominent theatre closer to his home. (He is from New Hampshire and my theatre was in Vermont.) The two shows ran for virtually the same dates, and he was up for the lead role of Stine in *Angels*. Could he have one day to get back to me about my offer?

I agreed to wait for his decision. He called me the next day, as promised, and told me he did receive the offer from the other theatre, and of course he needed to accept it. I agreed with his choice and I wished him well on the project. That actor played his cards well, communicated efficiently and timely between his potential employers, and never made me feel like he was blowing me off or disrespecting my production. His honesty and candor earned him my respect, which as an actor, he had hoped to maintain for future casting opportunities with me.

Furthermore, he made it a point to see a performance of *Cabaret* on one of his off nights. He found me after the show and offered his congratulations, expressing his eagerness to work with me in the future. And he invited me to attend a performance of *City of Angels*, leaving me with all the information about his show. (Remember: being seen in a production is as good as auditioning, if not better.)

In every way possible, this actor remained professional, and he ensured that he did not burn a bridge. All actors should follow his example in situations that require passing on work. The moral is, *Deal justly with everyone. You never know where you'll see them next.*

SUMMARY

- When you receive a job offer, gather all of the details and then say, "Let me think about it and get back to you" before making a commitment.
- If you cannot afford to take the work, try negotiating before making your decision.
- Consider what is to be gained or lost by accepting a particular job.
- Seek counsel from teachers or mentors before accepting work that would require you to join Actors' Equity.
- Before accepting a job, try to find out about the theatre and the director and decide if you really want to work for them.
- Do not pay to work at a theatre.
- If you must turn down work, be tactful and do not burn bridges. The industry is too small and insular to get away with it.

HEADSHOTS, RÉSUMÉS, AND COVER LETTERS

WHO COULD THAT ATTRACTIVE GIRL BE?

Beyond many schools and community theatres, virtually every audition you ever attend will require a headshot and a résumé. If you are serious about your career as an actor, you must acknowledge the photograph as a vital tool of your trade and a necessary investment. A photo session with a decent studio can run from $400, if you get a really great deal, to over $1,200; it's certainly not pocket change. But it is imperative that you find the photographer who is the best match for you and that you do not settle for someone who works cheaply.

Don't get me wrong, I'm not suggesting that only studios that charge $1,000 and up are worth their salt; some of my favorite headshots were taken very affordably. I am, however, urging you to hire a professional photographer who does *theatrical headshots*; do not simply have your dad or your friend take you out back with the digital camera for some free snapshots. I assure you, homemade headshots are *always* noticeably low quality.

So how do you begin to choose from among the hundreds of professional studios out there in every major city? What makes a particular photographer a good match for a given actor? My first piece of advice is to browse a photographer's work. They all have books compiling highlights of their repertoires; most now have websites as well. When you hear about a studio in the trade papers or through an online search, you should look at the style in which they shoot—each individual photographer has his own unique "look"—and you must ask yourself if that is the feeling that you are going for in your pictures. Find someone whose work appeals to you, first and foremost.

Another great way of shopping for a photographer is to talk with actors you know whose headshots you admire, and find out where they went. I've always found my network of friends helpful in recommending both whom to use and whom to avoid. I have even approached strangers at auditions if I liked their picture and asked who shot them. There are many resources available to you, so be selective.

As you narrow your search for a headshot studio, you may want to arrange to meet briefly with prospective photographers, if at all possible. You'll be spending a good deal of money on an afternoon with a particular individual whose job is to capture your essence on film. A certain element of compatibility is required to get you at your best, so you'll want to be sure you "click" with a photographer (pun intended) before you invest. The best cameramen are the ones who can effectively engage you in conversation and bring out your natural personality as they shoot you *candidly*, rather than forcing you to pose and smile. Some will even encourage you to bring your favorite music to the session. Their intent is to make you feel relaxed and comfortable so that the photos do not appear artificial. In general, a photo shoot that is fun for you will tend to be successful. So do yourself a service by finding a professional with whom you can have a good time and be your natural self.

PICTURE YOURSELF

So what should a headshot actually say about you? Over the years, trends in the industry have shifted: color versus black and white, smiling or serious, vertical or horizontal, head or full-body, and so on. But one rule remains fast: the headshot must be a representation of who you are. As a director, I must be able to assess a great deal about you from your picture and then have my expectations met when you walk in the door.

To begin with, *your headshot must look like you*. This sounds trite and perhaps even silly, but you'd be surprised how many actors, taken with the wonders of Photoshop, wind up with a picture that barely resembles their true likeness. Most photographers now offer free touch-ups when you purchase a session with them. These corrections should be limited to color and contrast issues, fly-away hairs, and minor blemishes that are not part of your everyday look. Be careful not to let them touch you up to look like someone other than you!

I will never forget an experience I had when I was casting a production in New York several years back and I received perhaps the best looking head-shot I've ever seen. She wasn't the most beautiful girl for certain, but the picture captured such a free-spirited, affable, and fun young woman that I almost wanted to cast her right out of the photograph. She was laughing and one of her hands floated up to her chest, as if we had just shared the most amusing joke or story together. I couldn't wait to meet her and encounter that effervescent personality firsthand. And would you believe it—at her appointed time, a girl walked in the door who I was certain had shown up in the wrong room. I asked her who she was, and when she responded with the name that was on the headshot, I didn't believe her. I held the picture up to examine its likeness side-by-side with the subject, and I felt utter disappointment in being misled by a photograph.

Mind you, this girl was not unattractive, nor would she have been turned away under normal circumstances; only, her headshot looked nothing like her! The hair was a different length and style, the skin tone was different in the picture, and the overall body type was greatly misrepresented in the picture. Needless to say, I didn't call her back. I can't even remember if her audition was any good. But I do remember her name. And I have kept her headshot in my file to use as an example of a great picture over the years. Be sure that the image you settle on captures *you* and not some idealized version of who you'd like to be.

Remember, these are *not glamour shots*. Unless you are going into the fashion magazine industry, your photo should not emulate a supermodel. To that end, you may want to be careful to avoid pricey studios whose fees include professional makeup and hair styling. They may help you to look beautiful, stylish, and glamorous, but they don't dress you and make you up before you leave your house each day; thus, it may be difficult for them to help you look natural in your pictures. It is often a better decision to put together your own look for your session, since you know how you present yourself to the world.

Your photographer will usually offer some clothing advice before you go to your shoot, but generally you'll be choosing your own outfits from your personal wardrobe. Whether you plan to include your body in the picture or simply to shoot from the neck up, you should select a variety of clothes in which you feel and look sensational. In particular, if you have specific features you consider assets (bust, hair, arms, etc.), be sure to bring attire that helps you accent these attributes. Observe yourself in the mirror wearing each possible ensemble option before you commit to any. What does the outfit accentuate or hide? What statement does it make about you?

You obviously want to avoid wearing ragged clothes, shirts with print or prominent logos, extreme white (it washes out on film), or distracting patterns. But beyond that, you want to be sure that you feel comfortable and confident in whatever articles you decide to bring with you. I would also avoid distracting jewelry, such as earrings or necklaces that draw attention away from your eyes and mouth.

During your session, you should be able to trust most of the work to the professional photographer. He will offer opinions on what looks or attitudes may work for you. He will ideally bring out the most in you, personality-wise. But you must never lose sight of the fact that you are the consumer. You are investing a small fortune in headshots that will serve as the calling card of your profession. You should have an idea of what you are going for when you arrive, and do not be afraid to speak up if you don't feel you are getting what you need. Most photographers are now shooting on digital cameras, which allow the client to view previews of her photos before the session is over. In these cases, it is imperative that you determine whether you have some viable options of images before you leave the studio. Demand your money's worth and don't settle for mediocrity. With studios that still shoot on 35 mm film, you won't really know if you got great results until you receive your contact sheets. However, it is still within your rights as a paying customer to request a reshoot if you are not highly satisfied with the work. It's always a good idea to discuss a photographer's policy on satisfaction guarantees before you make an appointment to shoot.

Once you do have your contact sheets (pages of thumbnail photos from your session) or a website or CD on which to view your session, you have an important decision to make regarding which images you wish to blow up to full size and reproduce. This is not a decision you should make on your own, nor is it a decision for your mother or your boyfriend or anyone else not involved in the theatre industry to determine. You should circulate your proofs among fellow artistic colleagues, mentors, teachers, and directors you know: people who know you well and also understand the business. These are the individuals who will help you narrow down the most appropriate photos for your purpose. (Not that your family's opinion isn't important, but parents usually tend to have a very different set of criteria on which they assess pictures of you. They usually gravitate toward the glamour shots.)

It seems to me that a mere 10 years ago, there was an unwritten yet rigid set of rules guiding the practice of headshot photography. Everyone used black-and-white film. Most were shot vertically for ease of flipping the page over to view the attached résumé. Rarely did actors use full-body or three quarter-length images—it was mostly neck-up. And the standard procedure was to have one smiling and one serious shot reproduced so that an actor could submit either, depending on the nature of the particular audition.

But, as trends shift, so have we all but done away with these outmoded theories of actor photos. Now, color is no longer taboo: most studios are shooting in full color since it is an equally affordable option, thanks to the digital age. The decisions to shoot vertically or horizontally, head or full body, are now being guided by the specific needs of the actor being photographed rather than by any industry standard. Long-legged, slender dancers may show more body and photograph vertically, while intense, expression-eyed actors may lean toward a horizontal, head-isolated-against-a-dark-background shot. Again, these are the types of choices you will make for yourself with your trusted counsel to guide you.

As far as the look you present in your headshot—serious or smiling—I offer this food for thought: directors are imaginative beings. Although you aren't beaming from ear to ear in your picture, I will assume you should be able to play a comical role. Likewise, if your submission captures you in a big, toothy grin, I will not disqualify you from consideration for a dramatic part. In short, you don't need a different headshot for every emotion in your range. (You certainly wouldn't submit a photo of yourself in a rage for the part of an abusive husband, I hope!)

Just choose one great shot that shows us an encapsulation of *you*. Be certain that your eyes really pop and gleam. And let your headshot really send a message to a director, either "You want to work with me," or "I have a secret and wouldn't you just love to know it!" If you present allure to ac-company your pretty face, then your picture will really work for you.

Finally, once you've selected your 8-by-10 image (and do be sure the headshot is not 8.5-by-11), it is important to choose a contemporary, stylish border and font for your reproductions. This is yet another expense that you mustn't scrimp on. Cheap reproductions are usually visibly low in quality, often overexposed, and always a surefire way to ensure that your photo session investment is wasted. Get a sense of what is current and popular in styles of borders—usually you can't go wrong with a medium black line against a white frame, but trends are ever changing, so ask the studio for input if you aren't certain. *Don't go with a borderless picture.* Also, be sure to have your name printed in the border of the photo in a clean, elegant font. Some people opt not to include their name on their picture, and this can make a director's job more difficult when weeding through actors and putting names with faces. The name you use when you work should be the name on your headshot. And the name on your headshot should match the name on your résumé. Many actors feel as though embellishing with their middle name will sound more formal and impressive, but I assure you that this is extraneous; just give us the name you would like to be called if we hire you.

Reproductions are sold in bulk quantities, so the more you order, the better the deal you will get. Be sure you get enough copies to suit your current needs for the year (Are you mailing out 3 or 4 per day or are you in college and only using them for summer work?). You can always order more, but you don't want to overshoot the mark, as any good headshot will need to be updated every few years, especially if you are young or you change looks frequently.

One other option to consider when ordering reproductions, especially if you had the hardest time deciding between two terrific images for your headshot, is a postcard. You may choose to have a second shot of you printed on a 4-by-6 card that you can send out to directors or producers either as a follow-up to an audition ("I really enjoyed auditioning for you, and I hope we get to work together.") or as an invitation ("I'll be appearing in a production of *Our Town*, and I hope you'll get a chance to come see it as my guest."). You have to run your acting career as a business in which you are the product being marketed, and correspondence is a tremendous part of that business.

Further on that point: I have several friends who have also created a business card with a headshot on it along with their contact information. You can do this very inexpensively on a home computer, and it can go miles toward making you look extremely professional. Imagine you are at a social event and you do not have headshots and résumés with you, but you meet a perspective employer or contact; you can offer her a business card and impress her with your preparedness.

Figure 7-1 shows the headshot of an actor who has done extensive touring and some Broadway work since finishing his MFA in acting recently. I include his headshot because it's clean and simple, and it represents exactly who he is when he walks in the door. This particular shot is black and white, which makes it more or less obsolete now, but for some reason it's worked very well for Aaron. As a director, I see this shot and I say: There's an interesting young man who strikes me as someone I would like to work with.

Aaron Galligan-Stierle

Figure 7.1. Headshot of Aaron Galligan-Stierle; photo courtesy of Joe Levy.

Figure 7-2 is another black-and-white photo, but I include it because of the style. Again, this looks exactly like the actress it represents. It sends a message that says: "I have a little secret and wouldn't you like to know." It's sexy without being overglamorous. Note how well the eyes are captured along with the soft mouth—this is very helpful to a director. Be sure that your face isn't in shadow and your eyes aren't squinting. Finally, I find that shots up against a wall tend to be very effective. I'm not sure why.

Figure 7-3 is a more contemporary style of headshot. It is in color, as most are nowadays. Note that it is horizontally set, or "landscape," as

Kirsten Rossi

Figure 7.2.   Headshot of Kirsten Rossi; photo courtesy of Kevin Fox.

opposed to the others, which were vertical. This type of photography usually places the actor to one side of the frame and crops very closely in on the head. My theory about why this is so appealing is that we are accustomed to television and film as our main sources of information and entertainment, and this is how we see faces on screen. As for the actor herself, this shot allows us to see her personality jumping off the page, and it represents her quite well. When Beth originally got her proofs, this shot was done against a stark white background. I suggested that she have the reproduction studio touch up the back with some color to set her apart, since she is blonde and fair skinned. This subtle tint to pink made a world of difference without losing any of the photo's quality.

Finally, figures 7-4 and 7-5 are examples of a postcard and a business card, respectively. Again, we get an effervescent actress who makes the director want to know her (she has a different, contrasting style picture for her actual headshot—the postcard allows her to follow up with a different look). Notice how she uses a landscape-style photo to fit the horizontal nature of a postcard, and she puts her name on the front. Also, notice how clean the business card is. It has all the information necessary without any clutter.

Beth Tarnow

Figure 7.3. Headshot of Beth Tarnow; photo courtesy of Laura Rose.

Figure 7.4.   Postcard of Erin Regan; photo courtesy of Tye Jakobs.

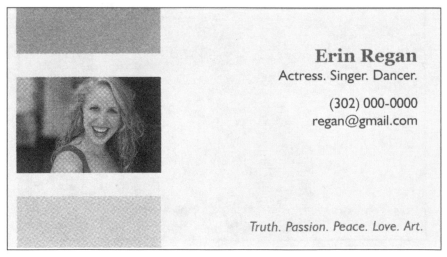

Figure 7.5.   Erin Regan's business card.

The Actor with Many Faces

It's an industry myth that every actor needs to have a smiling headshot for comedic and light auditions and a serious headshot for dramatic and heavy castings. I would much prefer an actor to choose one great shot that tells me who they are and sends a message (e.g., "You would just love working with me," or "I have a secret!"). Trust me to know that I can imagine you smiling or looking dramatic even if your headshot doesn't capture that.

As far as choosing multiple shots, I'm much more interested in your giving me a different style in a second picture, rather than simply a different pose. For example, if your main headshot is very urban, can you find a companion shot that's more boy or girl next door? If your primary picture is sweet and warm and welcoming, can you find a companion shot that's edgy and seductive?

Do you see how this type of contrast is much more informative than simply whether or not you are smiling?

The other consideration is whether a shot is "theatrical" or "commercial." These are two separate beasts, and an agent can guide you toward a commercial headshot if he chooses to submit you for film or print work. Suffice it to say that film shots tend to be urban looking, horizontal in layout, and very tight on the face, perhaps even cropped in at the top of the head.

As an actor, you will not want to consider using composite shots: These are 8-by-10 or postcard-size photos that contain two or more different poses of you on a card. Composites are used in the world of print modeling, but they are considered unprofessional for actors. Likewise, you probably want to avoid full body shots for theatre or film. We want to see a close-up of your face so that we really get the eyes and the lips without much other distraction.

WHO AM I ANYWAY?

The companion to your fantastically intriguing headshot is the clean, professional résumé, which will be stapled to the back side of the picture and trimmed to match the 8-by-10 size. Just as your photos require an investment of money, the résumé demands an investment of time and energy to produce an eye-catching list of credentials. It doesn't matter how much or how little experience you have; formatting your résumé well can impress a director by demonstrating your organization and professionalism.

Contrary to popular opinion, a résumé does not simply offer a laundry list of the roles you've played. It's much more informative. From your résumé, directors can get a sense of where and with whom you've trained and worked, what special skills you possess, even which jobs you regard highest in your personal history—an indication of your artistic values. In this unit, I will offer you some guidelines for creating a sleek, polished résumé that will impress, whether you are a high school student or a seasoned veteran. We'll also look at some examples in the pages ahead.

Any discussion on creating a good résumé must begin and end with formatting. I cannot stress enough the importance of proper spacing, handsome fonts, and clean lines. When a director receives your submission, he will glance at your photograph for a first impression, and then he will flip it over to read about your experience. Since time is always of the essence and yours is likely one of hundreds of résumés piled before him, he will want to be able to scan quickly down the page and learn as much as possible about you with minimal effort. You can help the director by making sure to choose a font that can be read without the aid of a magnifying glass. So many actors, insecure and desperate to show us *everything* they've done since birth, cram their résumés and choose a miniscule font size to fit it all in. Rule #1: Don't do this!

You will also want to become an expert on margins and the Tab key. As you add rows of information, it should fall into organized columns down the page. The spacebar will make you crazy, as it never lines everything up properly. Take your time and experiment with different fonts in order to get everything to fit the way you want directors to see it. You will notice that a 10-point Arial is a different size than a 10-point Garamond or a 10-point Times New Roman. So find the typeface that can be striking as well as functional for the amount of information you need to fit to the paper. It is also important to note that an acting résumé should *never* exceed one side of one page.

The choosing of a font and its size will likely not be finalized until you lay out the information and get a sense of how much space it requires. Be sure to continuously save your work as you go, so that you can experiment and not lose what you've already input. You'll also want to be able to access the résumé to make changes from time to time.

We'll step away from formatting now to talk about layout. The easiest way to discuss the proper organization of a résumé is to start at the top and work our way down. The résumé can be divided into several basic sections. While the specific information contained in each part will be dictated by level of experience, the headings and general ideas of each section should be fairly standard. Here are your general résumé subject areas, from the top down:

- Name and personal information
- Related experience
- Training
- Special skills

As I indicated, these general topics are standard across the board for actors from high school to Broadway. As we go through each heading, it's up to you to make it meet your personal specifications.

Name and Personal Information

The name on the résumé bears similar importance to the introduction at the top of an audition: It must state firmly, "This is who I am." Therefore, choose a larger, bold-faced font that will really jump out and catch the eye. I suggest utilizing the same font as you used for the name on your headshot, for consistency. You may want to center your name at the top of the page so everything below it will be spaced in accordance with the name. The other option that many actors choose is to put the name and personal information over to the left side of the page, leaving room for a small version of a second-look headshot to be printed in the upper right corner of the résumé.

"Personal information" is a catchall term for whatever details immediately follow your name and precede your experience. It includes contact information and vital statistics, but usually not much more than this. It generally begins, however, with a statement of what it is you do, followed by any union affiliations. If you have full musical theatre training, but you are primarily an actor, you might write "Actor – Singer – Dancer" underneath your name. Someone with a strong dance background who doesn't sing may choose to list herself as "Dancer – Actor," and so on. . . . The only rules for this line are that it must be the truth (if you do not sing or dance, just write "Actor" or skip this part altogether), it must not exceed three words (don't give me "Actor–Singer–Dancer–Musician–Acrobat"), and it should be in a smaller point than your name, usually about half the size.

If you belong to any artists' unions (Actors' Equity, Screen Actors Guild, AFTRA, etc.), you will need to list them on the next line down, centered beneath your name, using appropriate abbreviations: AEA (Actors' Equity Association), SAG (Screen Actors Guild), AFTRA (American Federation of Radio and Television Artists).

Next, list your contact information. Again, you'll want to keep this simple; the director doesn't need four phone numbers, three e-mails, and two mailing addresses. In fact, you shouldn't list a home address at all, unless there is a specific call for it with a particular submission. You will usually be sending your materials out to strangers, and sometimes it may be best if they did not have your residential location or your home phone number. Unfortunately, you may encounter people whose intentions are less than respectable. It's better to protect yourself and divulge that information only when you feel comfortable doing so. It's best to list only information that will remain permanent, so that a director can contact you a year after receiving your résumé if a role should come up; trust me, I do it all the time. A phone number and an e-mail address will be sufficient. Most actors usually offer their cell phone number so that they can be reached anytime, anywhere. Many actors living in cities and working professionally will choose to pay for an answering service. This is basically a line on which people leave you messages that you can retrieve by calling in from any phone, with a personal access code. A service is a great idea, especially if you travel with any frequency. It's inexpensive, reliable, and it lets you have an area code in the city in which you'll be based (e.g., 212 for NYC). Furthermore, it allows you to choose not to divulge your personal home or cell phone numbers if you wish to keep them private.

As a director, I love it when people list a cell phone *and* a service number on the résumé. This gives me the option of trying to actually reach a live person or, if I'm in a hurry, simply leaving the pertinent information as a message. Whatever phone number(s) you list, be sure to notate what type of line each number reaches: (212) 555-1747 (cell); (212) 555-2002 (svc.).

It's also a good idea to list an e-mail address in this technological age we live in. You should create an e-mail account that will be used solely for business, separate from your friendly, chatting e-mail or your college e-mail address. It won't cost you anything to start up an address with Hotmail, Yahoo, or Gmail, and it will help you distinguish career-related mail from everything else. I recommend the business e-mail be some form of your name, rather than a cute, catchy address that obnoxiously tells us how much you love Broadway.

Also, if you have a personal website that lists up-to-date performing credits, advertises upcoming projects, and displays headshots and production photos, you should list the web address here as well. Just be sure you're not providing a personal or untended site. A director might choose to look at it any time, and you'll want to be sure to maintain a current, professional appearance.

One note to college students about contact information: As you begin to send out submissions for professional work and attend auditions, it is so important to establish a permanent phone and e-mail contact. Do not list a college e-mail address, which will both expire upon graduation and also label you as a student. Use an address from one of the servers I mentioned above. And if you don't already own a cell phone, a service number is ideal for helping students make the transition from school to the city. Again, it will provide directors with a contact that will remain current even after you leave school.

After listing your contact details, leave a bit of space and provide your vital statistics. You'll want to list *height, weight, hair color, eye color,* and *voice part* if you sing. There is always debate about whether one should list weight on the résumé. As a director, I can tell you that it's very important that you do so. Think about it this way: I am receiving a photograph of your face from the neck up; I have no way of visualizing your body other than that. I need to know what physical type of person you are before I spend my time calling you in for an appointment; often I may be looking for a specific physical type to match my vision of a particular role. You *must* be honest about your height and your weight. If a director calls you in for an audition, he will expect to see what you have listed on your résumé, so don't put down what you wish you weighed, or how tall you think the role requires you to be. And if you are a person who changes looks at the salon from time to time, be certain to remain current with the hair color listed on your résumé.

You will notice that I did not include age, date of birth, or age range in this section. You automatically limit yourself when you offer your age to directors. Who cares how old you are? If you are 18 but can play 35, or vice versa, then your actual age is irrelevant. Don't get typed out before they see if you read right for a part. And as far as listing an age range, it is not for you to tell a director how old or young *you think* you can play. You'll almost always view yourself differently than others, so you're better served leaving that determination to the people casting the production.

Related Experience

This is the meat of the actor's résumé. In this section, or group of subsections, you will tell the director what shows and roles you have done, where you've performed, which significant artists you have worked with, and any other artistic projects you have done that may be germane to the particular audition for which you are submitting yourself.

I want to first offer you a few general suggestions about this section before we get into specific details. First, be sure to list your credits in *priority order* rather than *chronologically*. If you have worked with a well-known director or played a lead role or performed at a major theatrical venue, these credits should be listed prominently for more immediate notice. Second, *do not try to use four columns across the page to include the directors of every production you've done*. You run into small-font cramming, and the résumé becomes cluttered and hard to read. In the pages to come, I will address when and how to appropriately mention those great directors you want people to know you've worked with; in the meantime, just plan on a three-column format that will list show, role, and venue. Third, while it is imperative that you do not lie on your résumé, it's not a bad idea to remove taboo phrases such as "community theatre" and "high school." If you can find a way of listing a credit without drawing attention to the fact that it was amateur, it will serve you better. Community theatre experience can usually be manipulated by using the word "Players," as in "Williamsport Players" in lieu of "Williamsport Community Theatre." You can use the same trick for high school credits, but truly, you'll want to wipe high school and amateur performances off the résumé as soon as possible if you plan on being a professional artist.

Which leads me to the fourth general guideline: *Purge your credits now and then*. Many actors, hoping to impress with the exhaustive number of roles they have played, wind up with an excessively long (small-print) list of experience. Many of the roles—particularly those performed in educational theatre, where you rarely find age-appropriate casting—are no current indication of that actor's castability or type. And quite frankly, too many listings diminish the value of the few important ones. Show us what you've done, but don't overload us; quality over quantity, as the old cliché states. You may even alter your experience list depending on the nature of a particular audition. For example, list more musicals if you are going in for *The Full Monty*; more classical and nonmusical theatre if it's a Shaw or Chekhov piece.

The organization of your experience section will depend on the actual variety of experience you have had. It may be divided into subheadings to distinguish between different levels of working venues, but you should create a subheading only if you have two or more credits to list under it. If you are a beginner, you need only use one heading: "Theatre Experience" and "Representative Experience" are typically common titles for this section. If you wish to divide the unit into subgroupings to accentuate more of a range of work, you may consider the following captions to be used *when applicable*:

- Broadway (and/or) Off-Broadway
- Off-Off Broadway
- National (or International) Tours
- Regional/Stock Theatre
- New York Theatre (or Chicago, L.A., etc.)
- Professional Theatre
- Educational Theatre

Again, you do not want a section called "Community Theatre." It's an amateur red flag. If your experience is all or mostly in community venues, do not create a subheading under "Theatre Experience." Also, the "Educational Theatre" should be replaced credit-for-credit with each professional job you get in your postgraduate career. The only educational theatre credits you'll want to consider keeping are those roles for which you would be equally castable in the "real world."

As far as Broadway, Off-Broadway, and Off-Off-Broadway are concerned, I will remind you that these credits are based on the contract, not on the location of the theatre. In other words, if you appear in a show at the Producers Club, the American Theatre of Actors, or any of the other commonly rented venues around Manhattan, these are not considered Off-Broadway performances unless you are working under an official, union-sanctioned contract. I see a lot of actors label all their New York experience as Off- or Off-Off-Broadway to sound more impressive, but this miscategorization only makes an actor look ignorant, desperate, or dishonest.

However you choose to title headings and subheadings, you will want to either leave some space or indent below the heading and list each role in the three-column approach I mentioned before:

Title   Character   Theatre

The clean lines you create this way will let a director easily browse your list of credits with no confusion. In the event that a title or a theatre company exceeds the allotted space in your column, you have three options: abbreviate, change font or point size, or use two lines with an indentation. For example, *Picasso at the Lapin Agile* may be shortened as *Picasso . . . Agile*.

As long as you are neat and consistent, there is no absolutely right or wrong way to approach formatting. Note that play titles *always* go in italics, not in all capitals, not in quotes, and not underlined.

I've mentioned the notion of indicating significant directors or other artists with whom you've worked. The trouble with creating a fourth column for all of these names—besides the fact that it becomes an eyesore—is that as with listing too many acting credits, listing every director diminishes the importance of those few names you wish to stand out. A name buried in a long list may be lost; whereas, being selective about the frequency with which you drop names will give those you choose more emphasis. I usually recommend dropping down to the line underneath the title, indenting, italicizing, and using a slightly smaller font. Here are some examples:

Henry V	Pistol	Theatre Under the Sun
(Darko Tresjnak, dir.)		
Smokey Joe's Café	DeeLee Lively	Phoenix Productions
(w/ Gladys Knight)		
West Side Story	Riff	Struthers Library Theatre
(Spence Ford, chor.)		

I know that adding the extra line uses more space, but remember what I said about quality versus quantity? This approach is cleaner and it helps you really set out for a director those special collaborations that you wish him to notice. If you do your homework and you know who you are auditioning for, you may choose to alter your résumé, adding certain names which may provide valuable connections in particular instances. For example, if you know that the director has a history of collaborating with a choreographer whom you've worked with, throw that name on there. This is why it's important to staple résumés to the back of headshots as opposed to gluing or printing directly, so they can easily be removed and replaced when they require updating.

I told you this segment of the résumé comprised "related experience." I used this generic term because it is up to you to understand the nature of the audition and to determine what constitutes related experience. If you have film acting credits, you need only list them when submitting for a film role. However, for movie and television castings, you may still want to include your theatre acting work, since it's relevant to screen acting; just lead with your films since they will be of greater interest. If you are answering a general talent call for a cruise line (great work for young actors fresh out of school!) and you have theme park or similar variety performance experience, list it. But your role as a "Ferangi" at Paramount Park's Summer Star Trek Street Show is irrelevant when you go in for a production of *Carousel*. I speak from experience on this matter; I played the sci-fi character at a theme park attraction back in 1998. Theme parks are great summer work for a college student, since they pay you well to perform; however, they are usually not particularly helpful on the résumé when auditioning for legit theatre. Directing work and technical or backstage work of any kind is useless on the experience section of an acting résumé. Just list performing experience. Carpentry, stitching, makeup, choreography, designing, and other such talents can fall under "Special Skills," if you wish to list them. But remember, you are going for performing work. Your technical skills should be highlighted on a separate résumé that doesn't need to include your performance experience.

Again, a smart actor will not have one résumé set in stone for all purposes. The more experience you amass, the freer you are to tailor your résumé to make you more appealing for a specific project. This is where the computer word processor really earns its keep.

Training

In this portion of your résumé, begin by listing any and all degrees and certificates you hold and the institutions from which you earned them. You should even include nonartist education, such as a bachelor of science. It says something about you and your life experience, and it can be a great conversation starter (*I see you hold a degree in electrical engineering. How in the world did you end up being an actor?*) Do not list the year of graduation or intended graduation: remember, you don't want your age being a factor in getting or not getting auditions. Underneath each performer-specific training program, you may choose to highlight specific courses of study you took, such as Acting for the Camera, Ballet, Voice Production, and Stage Combat, although this is not absolutely necessary. What is vital, however, is a list of the faculty members with whom you studied.

In this business, whom you know is equally as important as what you know. If I recognize the person who taught your acting class, he or she may become a reference for you, which may give you an edge when auditioning for a play. All the more reason to maintain a good working reputation, even while you're in school! This business is small and directors will call around to get "the goods" on you.

Once you list all of your institutional programs, you can round this section off with any major workshops or private classes you've taken as a nondegree student. If you've attended master classes with well-known artists, you may choose to list a limited few stand-outs, but again, avoid clutter.

Special Skills

Finally, every résumé should include a *short* list of your special skills. The only absolute rule for this list is that you *must be able to do any-thing you include on it*, if requested. If you say you are a gymnast, be prepared to show them some flips; if you say you speak French, you'd better have a response to *"Est-ce que tu veux ce travail?"* And if you say you can catch grapes in your mouth, be ready to have some fruit tossed at your face!

This section of your résumé should list any talents you possess that are not evident from your experience (singing is not a special skill, but yodeling may be). If you have any unusual abilities, it may be advantageous to note them here. A sense of humor is usually not a bad thing in this area, as long as you don't overdo it. I have a friend who rounds his skills list off with: "And if you have a cookie, I will eat it." It doesn't always get him the job, but he's been known to get treats at auditions.

Typical examples of relevant skills include dialects and foreign languages, listed specifically; juggling, fire-eating, or similar clown work; in-line skat-ing; playing instruments; sight-reading; odd quirks, such as being able to touch the bridge of your nose with your tongue; contortionism; etcetera. A lot of actors list abilities such as driving (standard or automatic) and jogging, and I have yet to understand how these qualify as special skills. But I sup-pose if you are auditioning to play a guy who has to leg it home after his car breaks down on stage, these "talents" do come in handy.

But Look What I've Done!

Several of my students have asked me recently if awards and organiza-tions have a place on the résumé, for example, Alpha Psi Omega (Theatre Service Organization) or All-State Chorus. My answer is almost always no. While those sorts of accolades are helpful in the business world on a ré-sumé, and they certainly look good on a graduate school application, they do not help a director determine whether or not you are best for a role. The only exceptions would be specific major awards earned for theatrical or film performances (i.e., Tony, OBIE, Jefferson, Helen Hayes Awards).

More Than Meets the Eye?

Another question I was recently asked was in regard to weight on the résumé. A young actress was telling me that her true weight belies her appearance. She is a dancer and so she's all muscle, thus she weighs a good deal more than she looks. Should she put her true weight or the number that she more closely appears to be?

I'm never one for lying on the résumé; it's almost always a bad idea. However, this might be one possible exception. Remember, when you walk in the door you must be what the director imagined from your headshot and résumé. Therefore, if you truly look 110 but you weigh 125, there's no harm in writing 110 on the résumé. I would just make sure that you ask someone's outside opinion before deciding that you look 20 pounds less than you weigh.

The following pages contain a few sample résumés that demonstrate the different ideas I have set forth for you. The first represents an actor who recently finished college and has begun a career in New York, perhaps one or two years removed from graduation. The second is the more seasoned performer who has worked for a number of years on tours as well as in the city. And the third résumé belongs to a student in her second year of college. Each of the three samples is an amalgam of actual résumés I have in my file. I altered names and venues, but any of these could be legitimate, in theory. I also offer you several different formatting looks that can serve as templates for you to create your own résumé, whatever your level of experience. Notice that each one is formatted to fill the page handsomely, without overcrowding. All three are clean and readable, and each is a representation of where that particular actor is *currently* in his or her career.

TO WHOM IT MAY CONCERN

When you begin to answer casting calls in the profession, and likewise when you start applying to college programs, you will need to *include a cover letter with any headshot and résumé submission* you send out. Although in most instances its purpose is simply to say, "Hello, here's my submission," you mustn't underestimate the importance of a well-drafted letter, nor should you overlook its ability to make an impact. The cover letter can convey information not listed in the résumé, such as a current project that may be of interest to the director to whom you are submitting your materials. It

William Jefferson
Actor – Singer – Dancer

(917)555-2233 – Cell   (212)555-0111 – Svc.   WilJeff8@yahoo.com

Height: 5'11"   Hair: Brown
Weight: 188   Eyes: Green
Baritone

New York Theatre:

Comedy of Errors	Angelo	American Globe Thr.
Albert and Alice (workshop/premiere)	Albert	Chelsea Arts Forum
Side by Side by Sondheim	Man #2	Plaza Theatricals

Regional/Stock Theatre:

Forever Plaid	Francis	Weathervane Thr., NH
I Love You, You're Perfect...	Man #1	Tri-State Actor Thr., NJ
A Midsummer Night's Dream	Flute/Thisbe	NJ Shakespeare Festival
Romeo and Juliet	u/s Mercutio	NJ Shakespeare Festival
Death of a Salesman	Happy	Foothills Theatre, MA
My Fair Lady	Freddy	Mt. Washington Valley
Oliver!	Ensemble	Mt. Washington Valley

Educational Theatre:

Good News	Tom Marlow	Shenandoah Conserv.
Merrily We Roll Along	Franklin Shepard	Shenandoah Conserv.
Waiting For Godot	Vladimir	Shenandoah Conserv.
Twelfth Night	Feste	Shenandoah Conserv.

Training:

Shenandoah Conservatory – BFA, Musical Theatre Performance
    Acting: John Rolshe; Mickey Lee; Ted Ganter
    Voice: Susan Mendel; Pat Murphy
    Dance: Lena Jones (Ballet, Jazz); Fred Ingalls (Tap)

NYC Private Voice: Mary Swindell

Special Skills:

    Dialects (British, German, Irish, New York, Southern, et. al.)
    Stage Combat (certified)
    Piano & Trumpet
    Can belch or sneeze on command

Figure 7.6.   Résumé #1.

ANTHONY JASON ROGERS

AEA

The Flemming Agency: (212) 555-0909   Service: (212) 555-8183

Height: 6'2"   Weight: 175lb.   Hair: Black   Eyes: Hazel
Voice: Baritone

THEATRE:

--National Tours:

The Phantom of the Opera	Raoul	L.A./3rd. Nat'l. Tour
(*Hal Prince, Dir.*)		
Les Miserables	Enjolras	Really Useful Co.
(*John Caird, Dir.*)		

--Off-Broadway:

Berlin to Broadway	Tenor	Triad Theatre
w/Kurt Weill		
Riders to the Sea	Bartley	Theatre Three
Bedtime Stories	Halibut	Theatre Three
Rappaccini's Daughter	Giovanni	Wings Theatre

--Regional and Stock:

Carousel	Billy Bigelow	Garland Musicals
South Pacific	Lt. Cable	Garland Musicals
(*W/ John Raitt*)		
L'il Abner	Abner	Garland Civic Thr.
Guys and Dolls	Sky Masterson	Lake Highlands Thr.
She Loves Me	Kodaly	Trinity Theatre
No Exit	Garcin	Trinity Theatre
Twelfth Night	Orsino	Trinity Theatre
Arms and the Man	Bluntschli	Lake Highlands Thr.
Another Part of the Forest	John Bagtry	Lake Highlands Thr.

EDUCATION:

The Julliard School, NYC: MM, Voice Performance
Trinity University, San Antonio, TX: BM, Voice Performance
    TEACHERS: Liz Calvert, Tanzie Elridge, Cindy Hoffer, George Shaker
    COACHES: Rick Bardo, Stephen Hall, Mark Lovett

SPECIAL SKILLS:

Concert Pianist; Roller-blading; Dialects (list available upon request); Willing
to shave or dye hair & able to grow facial hair quickly

Figure 7.7. Résumé #2.

KATE LINDSAY

(954)555-1779
katiejo84@gmail.com

| Height: 5'4" | Hair: Brown | Eyes: Brown | Voice: Soprano |

THEATRE

Penn State University

A CHRISTMAS CAROL	Fan	Eisenhower Aud.
CHILDREN OF EDEN	Storyteller	Pavilion Theatre
(Workshop w/ Stephen Schwartz)		
NEW YORK ACTOR	Eileen	Studio 6

South Florida Theatre

SEXUAL PERVERSITY IN CHICAGO	Deb	Nova Southeast U.
OUR TOWN	Emily Webb	Taravella Players
FIDDLER ON THE ROOF	Chava	Taravella Players
ROMEO AND JULIET	Juliet	Taravella Players
SOUND OF MUSIC	Lisle	Opus Playhouse
HANSEL AND GRETEL	Gretel	Opus Playhouse

RELATED EXPERIENCE

- "Rebels Without Applause" Improvisation Troupe
  Member: 2003-2005
- *Coca Cola, International*—Commercial
  Eva Gorton Agency
- Miss Coconut Creek—Talent Contest
  Winner, 2005

EDUCATION

BFA, Musical Theatre: Penn State University (2010)
Private Voice: John Smith
Acting: Opus Playhouse; Theatre Co. of Plantation
Dance: Mrs. G's Dance Studio

SPECIAL SKILLS

Violin
Ice Skating
Cheerleading
Funny Faces

Figure 7.8.   Résumé #3.

may also draw attention to specific credits on your résumé that are directly related to the audition at hand. And, if nothing else, the cover letter can offer more of a sense of who you are: your personality, your intelligence, and your professionalism.

Most actors keep a basic letter saved as a file in their computer, a template that can be readdressed and modified with little effort. This framework should have a cordial greeting, perhaps a sentence or two on who you are and some highlights of your training and experiential background. And any letter you send out should *always* directly recognize the particular audition for which you are soliciting and why you feel you should be considered.

That last part is where a lot of actors get themselves into trouble, erring on the generic side and failing to be personal. When an actor sends me a letter like this—

Dear Sir or Madam,

My name is Joe Smith. I am an actor and a singer. I saw your casting call in *Back Stage*, and I was very interested in being seen for an audition. Enclosed, please find my headshot and résumé and feel free to contact me by phone or e-mail if it would be possible to set up an audition time.

I look forward to meeting you soon, and I thank you for your consideration.

Sincerely,
Joe Smith

—I can't help but feel that I am one of fifty recipients of the same exact mailing that day. How do I know the actor even read my specific casting breakdown? I took the time to lay out in detail exactly what I was looking for on my project, and this actor wouldn't take the time to acknowledge whether he even knew what that project was! In cases like this, I may glance at the photo and scan the experience, but you can be sure that Joe Smith will receive considerably less consideration than the person who writes this letter:

Dear Mr. Flom:

My name is Ben Becker, and I'm a New York actor. I saw your ad today seeking a cast for your production of *Forever Plaid*, and I hope that you will consider me for an audition appointment.

As my attached résumé will reflect, I hold a degree in musical theatre from Syracuse University, and I have a wide range of musical performing experience. Although I have never done a production of *Plaid*, I am able to sight-read

music, and I handle harmonies very well. My range as a bari-tenor makes me
an ideal candidate for the role of either "Francis" or "Sparky."

I very much hope I will have the opportunity to come in and sing for you.
Please feel free to reach me by e-mail or on my cell phone—both contacts are
listed on my résumé—if it would be possible to set up a convenient time to
audition. I look forward to meeting you.

Sincerely,
Benjamin Becker

Notice how much more appealing Mr. Becker becomes as a person, simply
because he took the time to read the casting call and to directly address
the needs of the audition in his letter. The second example is also personalized by the fact that he greets me directly. A director's or producer's
name is almost always included in a casting call ad. "Dear Mr. So and So"
is always advisable over the old "To Whom It May Concern" or "Dear Sir
or Madam." If there is no name listed on the ad, you may even begin your
letter with "Greetings" or "Dear Seaside Theatre." Do anything you can do
to diminish the impression that this submission is just another in your busy
week of mailings.

The other thing that is striking about the last letter is the fact that the
actor relates his skills and abilities directly to the production at hand. He
may know the show, or he may simply be responding to what the ad called
for. When I actually advertised for this show, I emphasized the importance
of sight-reading and harmony, in addition to breaking down each individual
character. This actor shows me that he understands the nature of the audition and he is interested in *my* production of *Forever Plaid*, not just any
audition he can get.

One final note about the Benjamin Becker letter: It is concise. He does
not go into a long-winded account of every musical he has done or every
teacher he has trained with. He does not turn the page into a kiss-up session, praising me as a magnificent director with whom he would be honored
to collaborate (you'd be surprised, but it happens). And he doesn't tell me
how it's "my lucky day to find the perfect actor" for my production (I'm not
making this stuff up!). He cuts to the chase, and he says exactly what he
needs to communicate to be appealing for this casting. That is the essence
of a good cover letter: Short and to the point, yet personalized. If you can
craft a good letter, you will find it gives you a certain edge in obtaining
audition appointments.

When it comes to applying for colleges or training programs, you will find
a more formal approach to your cover letter effective. These institutions are

more likely to be interested in your intellect and your writing skills, rather than just your talent and suitability for a particular production. Just as with a casting call, you would address your interest in the specific show, so should you understand and be able to express your desire in the specific school you are soliciting. Be sure to take the time to read any literature or websites available about a program; they are all unique, and some may be better candidates for your needs, as well as you for theirs. When you write to an institution, be sure to tell them why you are interested in their program, what appeals to you about their methods, their faculty, their reputation, and so forth. And tell them why they should be interested in you as well. What makes you an ideal student for the type of training they offer?

With school applications, grammar and usage are much more important than they are in the profession, where informality is acceptable and often welcome. Be sure to show your letters to a teacher or mentor for editing and input before you send them out. A guidance counselor usually knows what a college is looking for in a letter of interest, and they can help you to accent and highlight your attributes in an appealing, professional manner.

Unsolicited Mail

Sometimes actors will send out unsolicited mailings, usually to agents, seeking representation, or to production companies that are not casting a specific project at the moment, seeking future auditions. In these cases it is important to really research the agency or the company to which you are submitting yourself and tailor your cover letter specifically to what it is that they do.

We already discussed agents back in chapter 4, and how sending unsolicited mail to them usually leads nowhere unless you have a connection. Sending unsolicited mail to theatre companies may be much more useful to you. If you read in Back Stage that a company is seeking a production staff for their season, and they list the plays, some of which interest you, why not send them a letter of interest? Similarly, if you go on a theatre company's website and find their upcoming shows, why not jump the gun and submit a competent letter of interest before they hold open auditions? Remember, this is a business, so you need to be savvy.

I do suggest that rather than send out hundreds of headshots to every agent and theatre in the country for little or no response, that you be selective and find the companies that are best suited for your talents. You'll save time and money, and you'll increase your likelihood of a positive response.

The only other type of mailing you'll ever really send out will be the follow-up to an audition or the announcement of a performance. This is when having a 4-by-6 postcard with your headshot will come in handy. Once again, keep this short and sweet, but it's a great way to keep your name in the mind of a director. If there is someone you are very interested in working with, simply send him a postcard right after the audition, saying something like the following:

> Dear Mr. Jones,
>   Thank you for the opportunity to audition for *Carousel*. Please keep me in mind for this and future projects. I look forward to working with you.
>
> Sincerely,
> Amanda Arnold

If you have a current project, it would be a very smart move to invite the director, so list all of the performance information. Otherwise, just keep it to a sentence or two. The postcard may be slightly informal, and it is customarily hand written, as opposed to the typed business letter format of the cover letter.

I mentioned way back in our discussion on callbacks that you should have a notebook or a journal if you are to be a serious actor. The most important reason for the journal is to keep a running list of directors and casting agents with whom you've worked or for whom you've auditioned. When you are appearing in a production, you'll want to send postcards to anyone who might be able to come see you perform and may employ you later.

In general, the cover letter is another investment of time, as important as creating a powerful résumé or memorizing a book of songs. It is another tool in your arsenal as a working artist, and you must endow it with your voice and your personality for it to properly represent you. It is another method by which you can gain a competitive edge in this challenging industry.

SUMMARY

- Invest in professional headshots if you are serious about a career in the theatre.
- The headshot must be an accurate representation of who you are, not a glamour shot.
- Remember that you're a paying customer. Demand satisfaction from your photo session.

- Seek the opinion of theatrical colleagues, teachers, and mentors when deciding on which headshot to reproduce.
- Be sure to choose an attractive border and an elegant font in which to have your name printed on the headshot reproductions.
- Format your résumé so that all the information falls into clean, readable columns down the page.
- Do not choose a miniscule font in order to cram too much information on your résumé.
- Be sure to establish permanent contact information, such as a dedicated business e-mail address and a service or cell phone number, and list it on your résumé.
- Do not list age or age range on your résumé.
- List résumé credits in order of priority, not chronology.
- Use three columns across to list show, role, and theatre company.
- Remove the phrases "community theatre" and "high school" from your résumé.
- Select the few important, stand-out directors and choreographers you've worked with and list them below the credit, indented and italicized.
- Tailor your résumé for the given audition. What credits will be of particular interest to this casting? Place those credits high on your list.
- Be prepared to do anything listed under your special skills section.
- Always have your cover letters address the specific audition for which you are submitting.
- A good cover letter should be short, to the point, and personalized.
- When possible after an audition, send the director a 4-by-6 follow-up headshot postcard to *briefly* thank him for his time.
- Keep a running list of addresses of directors you've worked with or auditioned for and send out postcards inviting them to any productions in which you'll be appearing.

CONCLUSION

You've undoubtedly heard the odds against success in show business. You know that it's an industry of jaded cynics who must learn to deal with rejection as daily routine. And despite the enormous challenges that lie before you, you're determined to take a shot at it. To you I say: You can do it.

It's true that your audition-to-job ratio is likely to be easily 50 to 1 or even 100 to 1. But you know better than to accept it as judgment of your self-worth and to fall apart. You know that auditioning is your daily chance to perform, and that brings you joy. You understand that auditioning is not simply a means to an end; it *is* your career. And to you I say again: You can do it.

You will never know what the people behind the table are thinking—that they were looking for someone a little taller, a little blonder, a little less attractive. You can't know and you can't control it either. All you can do is commit absolutely to maintaining your vocal and physical instrument in top condition, studying and practicing the tools of your craft regularly, and being thoroughly prepared for any eventualities that may lie on your path to a career in the theatre.

Taking advantage of networking opportunities is never a bad idea either. While I believe that the saying "It's not what you know, it's who you know" is a bit overstated, it's certainly not without truth. This is why a good actor surrounds himself with other artists: playwrights, directors, producers, stage managers, and so on. It's an industry of friends, and people get work through word of mouth almost as much as by auditioning cold.

I would suggest however, that knowing the right people is only worth so much before you have to rely on what you know to carry you through. Below in a nutshell is the system I've laid out for you when auditioning for musicals:

- the repertoire book: fully stocked, neatly organized
- the entrance
- the exchange of information at the piano
- the confident introduction
- the performance, complete with smooth transitions
- the enthusiastic acceptance and application of directorial adjustments
- the gracious exit

If you make sure to apply this system, you are likely to note a more positive reaction from the artistic teams who see you. They will respond to your professional delivery. And though you will not always be cast in the end, you will find yourself attending a lot more callbacks. And, after all, that's the best result an actor can hope to achieve in an audition: the callback.

GLOSSARY

ballad: Simply put, a slow romantic or sentimental song.

belt: The common form of singing in contemporary musical theatre, often referred to as "chest voice." A woman produces this sound in the middle of her range where the bass and treble qualities can work together (starting at G above middle C). Think of it as a "calling voice" on a sustained pitch. It should feel very free, never strained. It is meant to emulate the sound of human speech more naturally than classical singing. Visit www.belcantocanbelto.com for more information.

callback: A follow-up to an initial audition.

cattle call: An open audition during which a large number of actors are seen very briefly. Sometimes they may "type out" or make decisions to hear or not to hear actors based on look, type, or special skills; for example, the director is only looking for blondes, men over six feet tall, or people with tumbling skills.

Equity (or Actors' Equity Association): The professional stage actors' and stage managers' union.

headshot: A close-up, professional photograph of an individual actor, used as a calling card at auditions. Frequently (though not always) shot in color film, from the neck or chest up. Often abbreviated as "pix."

ingénue: A naïve or innocent young female character type with a soprano voice.

juvenile: The male counterpart to the ingénue; typically a young tenor.

libretto: Also known as the "book," this is the spoken words, or script, of a musical.

monitor: The person who ushers people in and out of the audition room and/or keeps the sign-up list current and accurate. Occasionally, the monitor will also serve as a reader, providing the auditioning actor with a scene partner when reading sides.

open call: An audition that does not require an advance appointment. Generally, people either sign up for times in the morning or simply show up and are seen in the order they arrived. See also **cattle call**.

repertoire: The compilation of songs and monologues that an actor has *memorized* and *practiced*, for use in auditions. The songs should be neatly organized in a binder and brought to every audition.

rote: By memory; fixed or mechanical. An actor should know his audition pieces "by rote" so that he does not need to concentrate on remembering the words and can instead focus on acting choices.

score: The music portion of a musical, whether sung or instrumental; written by the composer.

sides: Short cuttings from the script used for an audition or a callback.

up-tempo: Usually considered the opposite of a ballad, this is a song style that moves at a quicker pace, with an "up" mood to it.

vamp: A short introductory musical passage often repeated several times before a solo or between verses.

REPERTOIRE GENRE LISTS

The following is a checklist of genres that make up a well-rounded repertoire. Here I also offer you a few select titles to get you started on your search, but don't limit yourself to the short list that I provide. As you continue in your training and your career, you should make every effort to have at least one piece that covers each genre. For musical genres, it's wise to have a ballad and an up-tempo for each. This way, you'll be prepared for any audition on short notice.

MUSICAL THEATRE REPERTOIRE GENRES

Operetta

"The Sun Whose Rays" from *The Mikado* (W. S. Gilbert and Arthur Sullivan)

"Poor Wand'ring One" from *The Pirates of Penzance* (W. S. Gilbert and Arthur Sullivan)

"I Am the Very Model of a Modern Major General" from *The Pirates of Penzance* (Gilbert and Sullivan)

"Summertime" from *Porgy and Bess* (George and Ira Gershwin with DuBose Heyward)

Jazz Standard

"Orange Colored Sky" (Milton DeLugg and Willie Stein)
"It's Only a Paper Moon" (Harold Arlen, E. Y. Harburg, and Billy Rose)
"At Last" (Mack Gordon and Harry Warren)
"One for My Baby (and One More for the Road)" (Harold Arlen and Johnny Mercer)
"The Man That Got Away" (Harold Arlen)
"King of the Road" (Roger Miller)
"Fly Me to the Moon" (Bart Howard)
"Stormy Weather" (Harold Arlen)

Pre Golden-Age Musical Theatre

"Let's Do It, Let's Fall in Love" from *Paris* (Cole Porter)
"I Could Write a Book" from *Pal Joey* (Richard Rodgers and Lorenz Hart)
"My Funny Valentine" from *Babes in Arms* (Richard Rodgers and Lorenz Hart)
"I Wish I Were in Love Again" from *Babes in Arms* (Richard Rodgers and Lorenz Hart)
"Falling in Love with Love" from *The Boys from Syracuse* (Richard Rodgers and Lorenz Hart)
"This Can't Be Love" from *The Boys from Syracuse* (Richard Rodgers and Lorenz Hart)
"Embraceable You" from *Girl Crazy* (George and Ira Gershwin)
"But Not for Me" from *Girl Crazy* (George and Ira Gershwin)
"They Can't Take That Away from Me" from *Shall We Dance* (George and Ira Gershwin)
"Our Love Is Here to Stay" from *An American in Paris* (George and Ira Gershwin)
"I'm a Stranger Here Myself" from *One Touch of Venus* (Kurt Weill)
"Mack the Knife" from *The Threepenny Opera* (Kurt Weill)
"Come Rain or Come Shine" from *St. Louis Woman* (Harold Arlen)
"Night and Day" from *Gay Divorce* (Cole Porter)
"I Get a Kick Out of You" from *Anything Goes* (Cole Porter)
"From this Moment On" from *Out of This World* (Cole Porter)
"I Wanna Be Bad" from *Good News* (B. G. DeSylva, Lew Brown, and Ray Henderson)

Golden-Age Musical Theatre

"You've Got to Be Carefully Taught" from *South Pacific* (Richard Rodgers and Oscar Hammerstein II)

"A Cockeyed Optimist" from *South Pacific* (Richard Rodgers and Oscar Hammerstein II)

"No Other Love" from *Me and Juliet* (Richard Rodgers and Oscar Hammerstein II)

"It Might as Well Be Spring" from *State Fair* (Richard Rodgers and Oscar Hammerstein II)

"Almost Like Being in Love" from *Brigadoon* (Alan J. Lerner and Frederick Loewe)

"If I Were a Bell" from *Guys and Dolls* (Frank Loesser)

"Lonely Town" from *On the Town* (Leonard Bernstein, Adolph Green, and Betty Comden)

"A Little Bit in Love" from *Wonderful Town* (Leonard Bernstein, Adolph Green, and Betty Comden)

"I Met a Girl" from *Bells Are Ringing* (Jule Styne, Adolph Green, and Betty Comden)

"Just in Time" from *Bells Are Ringing* (Jule Styne, Adolph Green, and Betty Comden)

"Always True to You (In My Fashion)" from *Kiss Me, Kate* (Cole Porter)

'50s/'60s-Style Rock Piece

"Falling" (Jerry Leiber and Mike Stoller)

"Hound Dog" (Jerry Leiber and Mike Stoller; performed by Big Mama Thornton or Elvis Presley)

"Can't Help Falling in Love" (George Weiss, Hugo Peretti, and Luigi Creatore; performed by Elvis Presley)

"Good Golly, Miss Molly" (Little Richard)

"Shop Around" (Smokey Robinson)

"Stupid Cupid" (Neil Sedaka; performed by Connie Francis)

"Runaway" (Del Shannon)

"Runaround Sue" (Dion DiMucci and Ernie Maresca; performed by Dion)

"Ain't Too Proud to Beg" (Norman Whitfield and Edward Holland Jr.; performed by The Temptations)

'60s-'70s Musical Theatre

"Arthur in the Afternoon" from *The Act* (John Kander and Fred Ebb)

"Colored Lights" from *The Rink* (John Kander and Fred Ebb)

"Much More" from *The Fantasticks* (Tom Jones and Harvey Schmidt)

"Simple Little Things" from *110 in the Shade* (Tom Jones and Harvey Schmidt)

"Wherever He Ain't" from *Mack and Mabel* (Jerry Herman)

"Time Heals Everything" from *Mack and Mabel* (Jerry Herman)

"Ribbons Down My Back" from *Hello, Dolly!* (Jerry Herman)

"The Other Side of the Tracks" from *Little Me* (Cy Coleman)

"Where Am I Going?" from *Sweet Charity* (Cy Coleman)

"Lost and Found" from *City of Angels* (Cy Coleman)

"Sara Lee" from *And the World Goes 'Round* (John Kander and Fred Ebb)

"I Don't Remember You" from *The Happy Time* (John Kander and Fred Ebb)

"Melisande" from *110 in the Shade* (Tom Jones and Harvey Schmidt)

"My Best Girl" from *Mame* (Jerry Herman)

"Put on Your Sunday Clothes" from *Hello, Dolly!* (Jerry Herman)

Musical Theatre Pop

"Spread a Little Sunshine" from *Pippin* (Stephen Schwartz)

"It's an Art" from *Working* (Stephen Schwartz)

"Spark of Creation" from *Children of Eden* (Stephen Schwartz)

"Stranger to the Rain" from *Children of Eden* (Stephen Schwartz)

"Holding to the Ground" from *Falsettoland* (William Finn)

"Change" from *A New Brain* (William Finn)

"My Friend, the Dictionary" from *The 25th Annual Putnam County Spelling Bee* (William Finn)

"I Think I May Want to Remember Today" from *Starting Here, Starting Now* (Richard Maltby and David Shire)

"The Story Goes On" from *Baby* (Richard Maltby and David Shire)

"Dancing All the Time" from *Big: The Musical* (Richard Maltby and David Shire)

"Waiting for Life" from *Once on This Island* (Lynn Ahrens and Stephen Flaherty)

"Times Like This" from *Lucky Stiff* (Lynn Ahrens and Stephen Flaherty)

"The Mason" from *Working* (Craig Carnelia)

"Proud Lady" from *The Baker's Wife* (Stephen Schwartz)

"Lost in the Wilderness" from *Children of Eden* (Stephen Schwartz)

"What Would I Do" from *Falsettoland* (William Finn)

"What More Can I Say" from *Falsettoland* (William Finn)

"Sailing" from *A New Brain* (William Finn)

"And They're Off" from *A New Brain* (William Finn)

"I Don't Remember Christmas" from *Starting Here, Starting Now* (Richard Maltby and David Shire)

"I Chose Right" from *Baby* (Richard Maltby and David Shire)

"I Want to Go Home" from *Baby* (Richard Maltby and David Shire)

"What Am I Doing?" from *Closer Than Ever* (Richard Maltby and David Shire)

"The Night that Goldman Spoke . . . " from *Ragtime* (Lynn Ahrens and Stephen Flaherty)

"Larger Than Life" from *My Favorite Year* (Lynn Ahrens and Stephen Flaherty)

"Love Who You Love" from *A Man of No Importance* (Lynn Ahrens and Stephen Flaherty)

Musical Theatre Rock

"Easy to Be Hard" from *Hair* (Galt MacDermot, Gerome Ragni, and James Rado)

"Where Do I Go?" from *Hair* (Galt MacDermot, Gerome Ragni, and James Rado)

"Donna" from *Hair* (Galt MacDermot, Gerome Ragni, and James Rado)

"Who Is Sylvia?" from *Two Gentlemen of Verona* (Galt MacDermot and John Guare)

"Night Letter" from *Two Gentlemen of Verona* (Galt MacDermot and John Guare)

"Inside Your Heart" from *But Boy: The Musical* (Laurence O'Keefe)

"Look at the Sky" from *Urinetown the Musical* (Mark Hollmann and Greg Kotis)

"I Believe My Own Eyes" from *The Who's Tommy* (Pete Townshend)

Pop-Rock (Be sure it can sound good when played on the piano!)

"Movin' Out" (Billy Joel)

"Just the Way You Are" (Billy Joel)

"Rocket Man" (Elton John)

"Levon" (Elton John)

"Lady Madonna" (John Lennon and Paul McCartney)
"Something" (George Harrison)
"Different Drum" (Linda Ronstadt)
"Blue Bayou" (Roy Orbison)
"You Took the Words Right Out of My Mouth" (Meat Loaf)
"I Feel the Earth Move" (Carole King)
"Landslide" (Stevie Nicks)
"A Thousand Miles" (Vanessa Carlton)
"Hit Me With Your Best Shot" (Pat Benatar)

Country/Folk

"Crazy" (Willie Nelson; performed by Patsy Cline)
"Desperado" (Don Henley and Glenn Frey)
"Cowboy Take Me Away" (Martie Seidel and Marcus Hummon; performed
    by Dixie Chicks)
"I Walk the Line" (Johnny Cash)
"The City of New Orleans" (Steve Goodman; performed by Willie Nel-
    son)
"I Will Always Love You" (original version by Dolly Parton)
"The Night They Drove Old Dixie Down" (Robbie Robertson)

Other categories to consider representing include the following:

- A Stephen Sondheim piece (only for use in Sondheim auditions!)
- A current Broadway or Off-Broadway hit
- A quirky, comedic character piece
- An obscure tune that no one is likely to have heard

MONOLOGUE REPERTOIRE GENRES

The following is a complete list for the professional actor. For the young
performer, having five monologues (classical comedic, classical dramatic,
great realism, contemporary comedic, and contemporary dramatic) will be
sufficient.

Classical, Greek or Roman

Medea; *Oedipus*; *Antigone*; *The Frogs*; *The Menaechmi*

Classical Verse Piece: Comedic and Dramatic

William Shakespeare; Ben Jonson; Christopher Marlowe

18th- or 19th-Century "Manner" or Restoration Piece

Molière; Richard Brinsley Sheridan; Oliver Goldsmith; Oscar Wilde; George Bernard Shaw

Early Realism or Naturalism Masters

Henrik Ibsen; Anton Chekhov; early August Strindberg (e.g., *Miss Julie*)

20th-Century American or European Realism Masters

Tennesse Williams; Arthur Miller; Clifford Odets; Eugene O'Neill; Brian Friel; Edward Albee; August Wilson

Anti-Realism

Bertolt Brecht; Samuel Beckett; Eugene Ionesco; late August Strindberg

Contemporary Realism or "Style Piece": Comedic and Dramatic

David Mamet; Neil LaBute; Paul Vogel; Lanford Wilson; John Guare; Richard Greenberg; Wendy Wasserstein; Tom Stoppard

Remember: read plays! And don't be afraid to get creative—you can cut and paste a monologue together for yourself by removing the other character(s). Just be sure that it makes dramatic sense and does not require an answer from an invisible partner.

B

SAMPLE REPERTOIRE BY ACTOR TYPE

In Appendix A, I offered you many song suggestions by genre. I will now offer you some more specific suggestions based on age, voice part, and type. Just be aware that these are only a few ideas to get you started. You should take the initiative to explore deeper and find music and monologues that really work for you. Also remember that you will need only a couple of representations from each genre.

BOOK 1: THE YOUNG INGÉNUE, SOPRANO

Music

"I Could Write a Book" from *Pal Joey* (Richard Rodgers and Lorenz Hart)

"Embraceable You" from *Girl Crazy* (George and Ira Gershwin)

"Down with Love" from *Hooray for What* (Harold Arlen)

"Falling in Love with Love" from *The Boys from Syracuse* (Richard Rodgers and Lorenz Hart)

"No Other Love" from *Me and Juliet* (Richard Rodgers and Oscar Hammerstein II)

"Cockeyed Optimist" from *South Pacific* (Richard Rodgers and Oscar Hammerstein II)

"A Wonderful Guy" from *South Pacific* (Richard Rodgers and Oscar Hammerstein II)

"If I Were a Bell" from *Guys and Dolls* (Frank Loesser)

"I'm Not at all in Love" from *The Pajama Game* (Richard Adler and Jerry Ross)

"Till There Was You" from *The Music Man* (Meredith Wilson)

"Mira" or "Yes, My Heart" from *Carnival* (Bob Merrill)

"That'll Show Him" from *A Funny Thing Happened on the Way to the Forum* (Stephen Sondheim)

"Hopelessly Devoted to You" from *Grease* (Jim Jacobs and Warren Casey)

"Simple Little Things" from *110 in the Shade* (Harvey Schmidt and Tom Jones)

"I Remember" from *Evening Primrose* (Stephen Sondheim)

"Much More" from *The Fantasticks* (Harvey Schmidt and Tom Jones)

"I Will Be Loved Tonight" from *I Love You, You're Perfect, Now Change* (Joe DiPietro and Jimmy Roberts)

"My Friend, the Dictionary" from *The 25th Annual Putnam County Spelling Bee* (William Finn)

"Blue Bayou" (Roy Orbison; style of Linda Ronstadt)

"Landslide" (Stevie Nicks)

Monologues

Measure for Measure (William Shakespeare); character of Isabella

Cymbeline (William Shakespeare); character of Imogen

Twelfth Night (William Shakespeare); character of Olivia

Much Ado about Nothing (William Shakespeare); character of Hero

The Three Sisters (Anton Chekhov); character of Irina

The Cherry Orchard (Anton Chekhov); character of Anya

Summer and Smoke (Tennessee Williams); character of Alma

The Last Night of Ballyhoo (Alfred Uhry); character of Sunny

Company (Stephen Sondheim/John Weidman); character of April

Women of Manhattan (John Patrick Shanley); character of Rhonda Louise

This is Our Youth (Kenneth Lonergan); character of Jessica

BOOK 2: THE YOUNG CHARACTER ACTRESS, MEZZO-BELTER/ALTO

Music

"But Not for Me" from *Girl Crazy* (George and Ira Gershwin)

"I Wanna Be Bad" from *Good News* (Ray Henderson, Lew Brown, and B.G. DeSylva)

"How Long Has This Been Going On" from *Rosalie* (George Gershwin and Sigmund Romberg)

"Blow, Gabriel, Blow" from *Anything Goes* (Cole Porter)

"I Wish I Were in Love Again" from *Babes in Arms* (Richard Rodgers and Lorenz Hart)

"I Had Myself a True Love" from *St. Louis Woman* (Harold Arlen)

"I Cain't Say No" from *Oklahoma!* (Richard Rodgers and Oscar Hammerstein II)

"It Might as Well be Spring" from *State Fair* (Richard Rodgers and Oscar Hammerstein II)

"I Can Cook Too" from *On the Town* (Leonard Bernstein, Betty Comden, and Adolph Green)

"Waiting for My Dearie" from *Brigadoon* (Alan J. Lerner and Frederick Loewe)

"The Gentleman Is a Dope" from *Allegro* (Richard Rodgers and Oscar Hammerstein II)

"Always True to You (In My Fashion)" from *Kiss Me, Kate* (Cole Porter)

"Something Wonderful" from *The King and I* (Richard Rodgers and Oscar Hammerstein II)

"A Little Brains, A Little Talent" from *Damn Yankees* (Richard Adler and Jerry Ross)

"Don Juan" (Jerry Leiber and Mike Stoller)

"Big 'D'" from *The Most Happy Fella* (Frank Loesser)

"The Other Side of the Tracks" from *Little Me* (Cy Coleman and Carolyn Leigh)

"You've Got Possibilities" from *It's a Bird...It's a Plane...It's Superman* (Charles Strouse and Lee Adams)

"Turn Back, O Man" from *Godspell* (Stephen Schwartz)

"The Miller's Son" from *A Little Night Music* (Stephen Sondheim)

"Colored Lights" from *The Rink* (John Kander and Fred Ebb)

"Lost and Found" from *City of Angels* (Cy Coleman and David Zippel)

"How Could I Ever Know" from *The Secret Garden* (Lucy Simon and Marsha Norman)

"Change" from *A New Brain* (William Finn)

"I Think I May Want to Remember Today" from *Starting Here, Starting Now* (Richard Maltby and David Shire)

"Look at Me Now" from *The Wild Party* (Andrew Lippa)

"Here I Am" from *Dirty, Rotten Scoundrels* (David Yazbek)

"I Feel the Earth Move" (Carole King)

"Natural Woman" (Aretha Franklin)

"How Do I Live" (Trisha Yearwood)

Monologues

As You Like It (William Shakespeare); character of Phoebe
A Midsummer Night's Dream; (William Shakespeare) character of Hermia
Antigone (Sophocles); character of Antigone
Othello (William Shakespeare); character of Emilia
A Doll House (Henrik Ibsen); character of Mrs. Linde
A Moon for the Misbegotten (Eugene O'Neill); character of Josie
Cat on a Hot Tin Roof (Tennessee Williams); character of Maggie
Beirut (Alan Bowne); character of Blue
Stop Kiss (Diana Son); character of Callie
Pterodactyls (Nicky Silver); character of Emma
Saint Joan (George Bernard Shaw); character of Joan
Key Exchange (Kevin Wade); character of Lisa

BOOK 3: THE YOUNG JUVENILE, TENOR

Music

"They Can't Take That Away from Me" from *Shall We Dance* (George Gershwin)
"I Can't Be Bothered Now" from *A Damsel in Distress* (George Gershwin)
"Night and Day" from *Gay Divorce* (Cole Porter)
"No Other Love" from *Me and Juliet* (Richard Rodgers and Oscar Hammerstein II)
"Almost Like Being in Love" from *Brigadoon* (Alan J. Lerner and Frederick Loewe)
"Younger Than Springtime" from *South Pacific* (Richard Rodgers and Oscar Hammerstein II)
"I Met a Girl" from *Bells Are Ringing* (Jule Styne, Betty Comden, and Adolph Green)
"I Believe in You" from *How to Succeed in Business without Really Trying* (Frank Loesser)
"Love, I Hear" from *A Funny Thing Happened on the Way to Forum* (Stephen Sondheim)
"Eve" from *The Apple Tree* (Jerry Bock and Sheldon Harnick)
"Johanna" from *Sweeney Todd* (Stephen Sondheim)
"The Night that Goldman Spoke at Union Square" from *Ragtime* (Lynn Ahrens and Stephen Flaherty)
"Larger Than Life" from *My Favorite Year* (Lynn Ahrens and Stephen Flaherty)

"Runaway" (Del Shannon)
"Something" (George Harrison)
"Landslide" (Stevie Nicks)

Monologues

Measure for Measure (William Shakespeare); character of Claudio
Othello (William Shakespeare); character of Roderigo
The Taming of the Shrew (William Shakespeare); character of Lucentio
Twelfth Night (William Shakespeare); character of Sebastian
Long Day's Journey into Night (Eugene O'Neill); character of Edmund
Summer and Smoke (Tennessee Williams); character of John
All My Sons (Arthur Miller); character of Chris
Picasso at the Lapin Agile (Steve Martin); character of Schmendiman
Burn This (Lanford Wilson); character of Larry
Snakebit (David Marshall Grant); character of Michael
Six Degrees of Separation (John Guare); character of Ben
Lobby Hero (Kenneth Lonergan); character of Jeff
SubUrbia (Eric Bogosian); character of Tim
Proof (David Auburn); character of Hal

BOOK 4: THE YOUNG CHARACTER ACTOR, TENOR OR BARITONE

Music

"I Could Write a Book" from *Pal Joey* (Richard Rodgers and Lorenz Hart)
"The Lady Is a Tramp" from *Babes in Arms* (Richard Rodgers and Lorenz Hart)
"Tchaikovsky" from *Lady in the Dark* (Kurt Weill)
"Brother, Can You Spare a Dime?" from *Americana* (Karen Lynn Gorney)
"You've Got to Be Carefully Taught" from *South Pacific* (Richard Rodgers and Oscar Hammerstein II)
"Once in Love with Amy" from *Where's Charley?* (Frank Loesser)
"Hey There" from *The Pajama Game* (Richard Adler and Jerry Ross)
"Joey, Joey, Joey" from *The Most Happy Fella* (Frank Loesser)
"Just in Time" from *Bells Are Ringing* (Jule Styne, Betty Comden, and Adolph Green)
"All I Need Is the Girl" from *Gypsy* (Jule Styne and Stephen Sondheim)
"Bring Me My Bride" from *A Funny Thing Happened on the Way to the Forum* (Stephen Sondheim)

"Melisande" from *110 in the Shade* (Harvey Schmidt and Tom Jones)
"Leaning on a Lamppost" from *Me and My Girl* (Noel Gay)
"Sara Lee" (John Kander and Fred Ebb)
"The Mason" from *Working* (Craig Carnelia)
"And They're Off" from *A New Brain* (William Finn)
"One Night with You" (Elvis Presley)

Monologues

Cymbeline (William Shakespeare); character of Cloten
King Lear (William Shakespeare); character of Edmund
Much Ado about Nothing (William Shakespeare); character of Dogberry
Comedy of Errors (William Shakespeare); character of Antipholus of Ephesus
Long Day's Journey into Night (Eugene O'Neill); character of Jamie
Death of a Salesman (Arthur Miller); character of Happy or Biff
The Three Sisters (Anton Chekhov); character of Solyony
A Doll House (Henrik Ibsen); character of Krogstad
Snakebit (David Marshall Grant); character of Jonathan
Beirut (Alan Bowne); character of Torch
The Last Night of Ballyhoo (Alfred Uhry); character of Joe
Fat Pig (Neil LaBute); character of Carter
Burn This (Lanford Wilson); character of Pale
Picasso at the Lapin Agile (Steve Martin); character of Picasso
Key Exchange (Kevin Wade); character of Philip
Art (Yasmina Reza); character of Yvan

BOOK 5: THE LEADING LADY

Music

"Bill" from *Show Boat* (Jerome Kern and Oscar Hammerstein II)
"My Ship" from *Lady in the Dark* (Kurt Weill)
"Come Rain or Come Shine" from *St. Louis Woman* (Harold Arlen)
"No Other Love" from *Me and Juliet* (Richard Rodgers and Oscar Hammerstein II)
"So in Love" from *Kiss Me, Kate* (Cole Porter)
"I'm Going Back" from *Bells Are Ringing* (Jule Styne, Betty Comden, and Adolph Green)
"Maybe This Time" from *Cabaret* (John Kander and Fred Ebb)

"Unusual Way" from *Nine* (Arthur Kopit and Maury Yeston)
"Someone Else's Story" from *Chess* (Benny Andersson and Bjorn Ulvaeus)
"Lost and Found" from *City of Angels* (Cy Coleman and David Zippel)
"Holding to the Ground" from *Falsettoland* (William Finn)
"The Story Goes On" from *Baby* (Richard Maltby and David Shire)
"Back to Before" from *Ragtime* (Lynn Ahrens and Stephen Flaherty)
"Willing to Ride" from *Steel Pier* (John Kander and Fred Ebb)
"You Don't Know This Man" from *Parade* (Jason Robert Brown)
"Natural Woman" (Aretha Franklin)
"I Feel the Earth Move" (Carole King)
"Both Sides Now" (Joni Mitchell)

Monologues

The Winter's Tale (William Shakespeare); character of Hermione
Henry IV, Part II (William Shakespeare); character of Lady Percy
Merchant of Venice (William Shakespeare); character of Portia
Taming of the Shrew (William Shakespeare); character of Katherina
Much Ado about Nothing (William Shakespeare); character of Beatrice
Medea (Euripides); character of Medea
The Cherry Orchard (Anton Chekhov); character of Ranevskaya
Ghosts (Henrik Ibsen); character of Mrs. Alving
A Streetcar Named Desire (Tennessee Williams); character of Blanche
All My Sons (Arthur Miller); character of Ann
Proof (David Auburn); character of Claire
Women of Manhattan (John Patrick Shanley); character of Billie
Life x 3 (Yasmina Reza); character of Sonia
The Goat, or Who Is Sylvia? (Edward Albee); character of Stevie
Saint Joan (George Bernard Shaw); character of Joan

BOOK 6: THE LEADING MAN

Music

"Embraceable You" from *Girl Crazy"* (George and Ira Gershwin)
"Make Believe" from *Show Boat* (Jerome Kern and Oscar Hammerstein II)
"My Romance" from *Jumbo* (Richard Rodgers and Lorenz Hart)
"I've Got the World on a String" from *Cotton Club Paradise* (Harold Arlen)
"Lucky to Be Me" from *On the Town* (Leonard Bernstein, Betty Comden, and Adolph Green)

"There But for You Go I" from *Brigadoon* (Alan J. Lerner and Frederick Loewe)

"So in Love" from *Kiss Me, Kate* (Cole Porter)

"Were Thine That Special Face" from *Kiss Me, Kate* (Cole Porter)

"This Nearly Was Mine" from *South Pacific* (Richard Rodgers and Oscar Hammerstein II)

"I've Never Been in Love Before" from *Guys and Dolls* (Frank Loesser)

"They Call the Wind Maria" from *Paint Your Wagon* (Alan J. Lerner and Frederick Loewe)

"I Met a Girl" from *Bells Are Ringing* (Jule Styne, Betty Comden, and Adolph Green)

"If Ever I Would Leave You" from *Camelot* (Alan J. Lerner and Frederick Loewe)

"What Kind of Fool Am I" from *Stop the World—I Want to Get Off* (Leslie Bricusse and Anthony Newley)

"Marry Me" from *The Rink* (John Kander and Fred Ebb)

"Melisande" from *110 in the Shade* (Harvey Schmidt and Tom Jones)

"Anthem" from *Chess* (Benny Andersson and Bjorn Ulvaeus)

"The Day After That" from *Kiss of the Spider Woman* (John Kander and Fred Ebb)

"Sailing" from *A New Brain* (William Finn)

"She's Got a Way" (Billy Joel)

Monologues

Henry V (William Shakespeare); character of Henry
Othello (William Shakespeare); character of Cassio
Much Ado about Nothing (William Shakespeare); character of Benedick
Twelfth Night (William Shakespeare); character of Orsino
A Doll House (Henrik Ibsen); character of Torvald
An Enemy of the People (Henrik Ibsen); character of Peter Stockmann
The Cherry Orchard (Anton Chekhov); character of Lophokhin
Cat on a Hot Tin Roof (Tennessee Williams); character of Brick
All My Sons (Arthur Miller); character of Chris
Oleanna (David Alan Mamet); character of John
Women of Manhattan (John Patrick Shanley); character of Duke
Six Degrees of Separation (John Guare); character of Paul
M. Butterfly (David Henry Hwang); character of Gallimard
Art (Yasmina Reza); character of Serge
Burn This (Lanford Wilson); character of Burton

SOME RECOMMENDED DOS AND DON'TS

Some final, random suggestions . . .

DO

- Be creative and piece together monologues from larger scenes.
- Think outside the box for song choices.
- Bring a sense of humor into every audition (without overdoing it).
- Keep in good contact with any writers, directors, or stage managers whom you know—you never know when they'll be in a position to get you work.
- Feel free to use a song out of context or in a different style to suit a particular audition (e.g., "Brother, Can You Spare a Dime?" swung, as a vaudevillian striptease for a Cabaret audition).
- Look at great musical libretti for monologues—they're often over-looked gems (e.g., *Company* or *Assassins*).
- Bring any song you're going to add to your repertoire to an accompanist or vocal coach to ensure that it's marked well and easy to sight read.
- Cut your pieces so that you show them just what they need to see.

DON'T

- Write your own monologue for an audition.
- Use a monologue that is not from a play.
- Sing Sondheim songs at an audition, unless you're auditioning for a Sondheim show.
- Experiment at auditions (e.g., try out a new song that you've never sung before).
- Use a monologue from a film to audition for theatre.
- Audition with props unless you are auditioning to be a prop act.
- Try to show a wide range of emotions (e.g., "can cry at will") simply for the sake of showing them.
- Accept not being called back or cast as a judgment of your self-worth.
- Carry an audition around with you emotionally or mentally after the fact; just let it go.

INDEX

ABOUT THE AUTHOR

Jonathan Flom is an assistant professor of theatre at Shenandoah Conservatory in Winchester, Virginia. He teaches courses in acting, directing, and musical theatre, and he directs the musical productions. Before coming to Shenandoah, Flom headed the theatre minor at Lyndon State College in "the sticks" of Vermont, where he wrote, administered, and taught the theatre curriculum. There, he also found the time to write this book.

Flom is a proud alumnus of Penn State University, where he was the first candidate to earn an MFA degree in directing for the musical theatre stage. He also holds a BFA in musical theatre from Penn State.

Flom has worked as a freelance director in New York City as well as Chicago, New Jersey, Connecticut, and Vermont. His professional credits include Goodspeed Musicals, Tri-State Actors Theatre, First Street Playhouse, American Theatre of Actors, and Struthers Library Theatre.

The audition technique set forth in this book was developed over several years in State College, New York, and Chicago, and is now available as a master class for high schools and colleges. Contact actorcoach@hotmail.com for more information.